Science in Progress

MORE

Articles from Smithsonian Magazine's Smart News

Keiko Miyamoto

KINSEIDO

Kinseido Publishing Co., Ltd.

3-21 Kanda Jimbo-cho, Chiyoda-ku,
Tokyo 101-0051, Japan

First published 2023 by Kinseido Publishing Co., Ltd.

Text design　Asahi Media International Inc.

🎧 音声ファイル無料ダウンロード

https://www.kinsei-do.co.jp/download/4185

この教科書で 🎧 DL 00 の表示がある箇所の音声は、上記 URL または QR コードにて無料でダウンロードできます。自習用音声としてご活用ください。

- ▶ PC からのダウンロードをお勧めします。スマートフォンなどでダウンロードされる場合は、**ダウンロード前に「解凍アプリ」をインストール**してください。
- ▶ URL は、**検索ボックスではなくアドレスバー (URL 表示覧)** に入力してください。
- ▶ お使いのネットワーク環境によっては、ダウンロードできない場合があります。

🔘 **CD 00**　左記の表示がある箇所の音声は、教室用 CD（Class Audio CD）に収録されています。

はしがき

　本書はアメリカの国立学術文化研究機関であるスミソニアン協会がオンラインで発行している *Smithsonian Magazine* の Smart News を元にした英語教材です。2020年に出版した *Science at Hand* の続編になります。Smart News の特徴は、サイエンス誌やネイチャー誌をはじめとする一流論文誌に掲載された最先端の研究を、サイエンスライターの手により、わかりやすく簡潔にまとめていることです。すべての記事には裏付けがあり、ニュースソースの新聞、雑誌の記事や論文などにリンクが貼ってあることも、科学記事としての信頼性を高めているといえます。

　今回は脳科学、ロボット工学、機械工学、化学工学、環境科学、人間行動学、絵画、ファッションなど幅広い分野から、私たちの生活に関わりのある興味深い最新のニュースを15本選びました。

　日本語による導入から始まる各Unitは、次のような構成になっています。

Before You Read

　空所に適切な英語や日本語を入れる演習です。Unitに登場する重要な単語・表現を学びます。

Reading

　学習に適した400～500語の長さに編集した記事の原文です。Notes（主として語注）とExtra Notes（簡単な事項説明）を付しました。

Comprehension Questions

　🅐は記事の内容に一致するかどうかを問う T/F 問題、🅑は穴埋め問題を解きながら要約文を完成させた後、音声を聞いて答えを確認する問題になっています。

Read Better, Understand More!

　科学分野の記事の理解に役立つ文法を解説し、理解度確認の Exercise を設けました。

After You Read

　🅐では Reading で読んだ記事に関する、男女2人の会話を聞いて空所を埋めた後、会話練習を行います。続く🅑で、今回初めて簡単な作文演習が登場します。自分の言葉で空所を埋める作業です。

Behind the Scenes

　各テーマの理解に役立つ情報のコラムです。

　学生のみなさんが英文科学記事を読む喜びを知り、読み続ける習慣を身に付け、知らず知らずのうちに英語力を高めていく。そんなプロセスに本書が少しでも役立つことを願っています。

　最後になりましたが、今回も金星堂編集部のみなさまに大変お世話になりましたことを心より感謝いたします。

　　　　　　　　　　　　　　　　　　　　　　　　　　　　　　　　宮本惠子

Contents

UNIT 1

短時間の昼寝により生産性が高まる、とはよく言われることですが、昼寝のやり方次第で、創造性も高まることがこのほどパリ脳研究所の研究でわかりました。トーマス・エジソンやサルバドール・ダリがすでに実践していたと言われるこの眠りのテクニック。その鍵は、創造的眠りのスイートスポットと呼ばれる領域です。

" Need a Creative Boost? Nap Like Thomas Edison and Salvador Dalí "

Before You Read

A 日本語の意味に合うように、空所に適切な語を語群から選んで書きましょう。語群には1つ余分なものがあります。

1. 発明家のエジソンはひらめきが必要になると特別なテクニックを用いた
when (   ) Edison needed inspiration, he adopted a special technique

2. 覚醒と睡眠のちょうど中間にあるぼんやりした段階
the hazy stage right between (   ) and sleep

3. ヒプナゴジアは創造性を刺激することができる
hypnagogia can (   ) creativity

4. 16名の参加者はその暗号を解いた
sixteen participants (   ) the code

5. 彼らにはさらに問題が与えられた
they were (   ) more questions

> cracked inventor spark consciousness predicted assigned

B 下線部の英語の意味として適切な日本語を空所に書きましょう。

1. access <u>inaccessible</u> elements   (   ) 要素にアクセスする

2. <u>sleep break</u> refreshed people's brains   (   ) が人々の脳をリフレッシュした

3. semi-aware of their <u>surroundings</u>   (   ) を半ば意識している

4. people can let their thoughts <u>drift</u>   人々は考えを (   ) ことができる

5. the <u>everyday person</u> can try out   (   ) が試すことができる

Reading

Notes

1 When artist Salvador Dalí and inventor Thomas Edison needed inspiration, they adopted a similar, bizarre sleeping technique. They tried to sleep while holding a small object in their hands, which would then clatter to the floor and wake
5 them up just as they started to doze off. When they woke, they'd go straight to work, Yasemin Saplakoglu reports for *Live Science*.

2 It turns out that Dalí and Edison were onto something by letting their brains slip gently into the first phase of sleep,
10 but no further. A new study published last week in *Science Advances* suggests that the hazy stage right between consciousness and sleep—called N1 or hypnagogia—can spark creativity, Clare Wilson reports for *New Scientist*.

3 To investigate the science behind Dalí and Edison's sleep
15 technique, Delphine Oudiette, a neuroscientist at the Paris Brain Institute and her collaborators gave a set of math problems to 103 participants, and the key to solving them was a hidden pattern. Sixteen participants cracked the code and solved the problems immediately, but the rest were told
20 to take a 20-minute break in which they were hooked up to a machine that monitors brain waves, *Scientific American* reports.

4 Just like Dalí and Edison, they got comfortable and held an object in their hands. Once the 20 minutes were up, they
25 were told to record what thoughts they had while they were asleep. Then, they were assigned more questions. Nearly 83 percent of the participants who reached hypnagogia solved the hidden pattern and answered the questions. Only 31 percent of people who stayed awake and 14 percent of those
30 who progressed to a deeper level of sleep managed to solve the problems, *New Scientist* reports.

5 "The new results suggest there is a creative sleep sweet spot during which individuals are asleep enough to access otherwise inaccessible elements but not so far gone that the

bizarre　奇妙な

clatter to　～に当たってカタカタ鳴る（音をたてる）
doze off　うとうとと眠り込む

Live Science　科学ニュースを発信しているウェブサイト
onto something
いいところに気づく
slip into　いつの間にか～の状態になる（陥る）

New Scientist
科学技術分野の情報を解説する英語の週刊科学雑誌
neuroscientist　神経科学者
Paris Brain Institute
パリ脳研究所
collaborator　共同研究者

hook up to　～につなぐ

Scientific American
世界最古の一般向け科学雑誌

material is lost," Jonathan Schooler, a psychologist at the
University of California, Santa Barbra who was not involved
in the study, tells *Scientific American*. However, the sleep
break could have also refreshed some people's brains,
allowing them to come back and solve the problems with
clearer minds, he says.

6 Why the N1 stage is the "creative sleep sweet spot" is
still unclear. Oudiette tells *Live Science* that it could be
because people are still at least semi-aware of their
surroundings but can also let their thoughts drift, creating a
state of "loose cognition and weird associations." Plus, "[you]
also have the ability to catch it if you get a good idea."

7 In the future, Oudiette hopes to figure out how people
could access this creative sweet spot without having to hold
an object to wake them up. But in the meantime, it's an
experiment that the everyday person can try out at home,
Live Science reports.

Notes

cognition　認知力
weird　風変わりな
association　連想

Extra Notes

l. 10 *Science Advances*：米国科学振興協会（AAAS）が幅広い分野を対象にオンライン版のみで発行しているオープンアクセス雑誌　*l.* 12 hypnagogia：ヒプナゴジア、覚醒状態から睡眠状態への移行（入眠）時における半覚醒状態

Comprehension Questions

A 記事の内容に一致するものには T（True）、一致しないものには F（False）に丸をつけ、判断の基準になったパラグラフの番号を（ ）に書き込みましょう。ただし、基準とするパラグラフは複数ある場合もあります。

1. Oudiette is afraid that the only way people could access this creative sweet spot is to hold an object to wake them up.　　**T / F**　（　　　）

2. The new results suggest there is a creative sleep sweet spot, and the researchers have found out the reason why the N1 stage is the "creative sleep sweet spot."　　**T / F**　（　　　）

3. The participants who reached hypnagogia showed better performance in solving the hidden pattern than those people who stayed awake, or progressed to a deeper level of sleep.
　　T / F　（　　　）

4. Eighty-seven participants were very uncomfortable during a 20-minute break since they were hooked up to a machine that monitors brain waves.　　**T / F**　（　　　）

5. Dalí and Edison got inspiration from N1 or hypnagogia, the hazy stage right between consciousness and sleep.　　**T / F**　（　　　）

B 以下は記事の要約です。適切な語を空所に書き入れ、音声を聞いて答えを確認しましょう。

🎧 DL 02　　💿 CD 1-09

　　The (**b**　　　　　^{1}) sleeping technique (**a**　　　　　^{2}) by artist Salvador Dalí and (**i**　　　　　^{3}) Thomas Edison was (**i**　　　　　^{4}) by the researchers at the Paris Brain Institute. The study (**p**　　　　　^{5}) last week suggests that the hazy stage between consciousness and sleep—called N1—can (**s**　　　　　^{6}) creativity and there exists a (**c**　　　　　^{7}) sleep sweet spot, during which people are half (**a**　　　　　^{8}) and half aware, producing a state of "loose (**c**　　　　　^{9}) and weird (**a**　　　　　^{10})."

Read Better, Understand More!

冠詞

　英語の冠詞って少し日本語の「てにをは」（助詞）に通じるところがあり、あってもなくても大体の意味は通じるようで、実は重要な役割を果たしています。たとえば初対面の人がいきなり「私が青木です」と言ったら、あなたは面食らってしまいますよね。それは「が」という助詞が、すでに「青木」という人についての情報をあなたが持っている、ということを暗に示しているからです。

　aと theについても全く同じことが言えます。
This is an apple. は「（たくさんあるうちの1個の）りんご」という新しい情報を示しています。
This is the apple. は「そのりんご」についての情報をすでに読者が持っていて、「そのりんご」は「唯一」の存在であることを示しています。

　それでは、本文中のaと theについて振り返ってみましょう。次の例を見てください。
holding a small object in their hands, which would then clatter to the floor
「（彼らは）小さな物を手に握っているが、それが床に落ちコトンと音をたてる」

　small objectも floorも初出の単語ですが、the floorとすることで、手に持った物体が落ちてぶつかる「その床」はそこに1枚しかないことが読者に伝わります。では、ここでtheの代わりにaが使われていたらどういうニュアンスになるのでしょうか？　「いくつもある床のどれか」に落ちて音をたてることになり、まるで床が1つではない、多次元ワールドで起こるような話になってしまいます。

　次の例を見てください。
Delphine Oudiette, a neuroscientist at the Paris Brain Institute
「パリ脳研究所の神経科学者（である）デルフィン・ウディエット」

　aが使われているのは、Paris Brain Instituteには複数の神経科学者が働いていて、Delphine Oudietteは「その中の1人」だからです。

Exercise

次の空所に適切な冠詞を入れましょう。

1. Yokohama is (　　　　　　　　　) name of (　　　　　　　　　) city in Japan.

2. I am (　　　　　　　　) student at ABC University.

3. Give me (　　　　　　　) apple.
（八百屋の店先でりんごを指差しながら言うセリフ）

After You Read

DL 03   CD 1-10

A 会話を聞き、空所を埋めましょう。その後、会話をペアで練習しましょう。

Evan: I'm so tired. I have to write a 20-page essay ¹_____
_____ by tomorrow morning, but I have brain fog and can't think
of any ideas at all.

Julia: ²_____ a coffee to clear your head?

Evan: That's very kind of you, but I've had enough coffee already.

Julia: Well, then, why don't you try Salvador Dalí's unique sleeping technique?
He ³_____ the N1 stage of sleep, that is the hazy stage
⁴_____, in order to
spark creativity.

Evan: Hmm, that sounds interesting. But how can I do that?

Julia: Try to sleep while holding ⁵_____.
When you start to doze off, the object will clatter to the floor to wake you up.

B 以下の①と②の問題に答えましょう。

① 以下の例を見て、自分の言葉で文章の空所を埋めましょう。

    ex) Would you like to try Salvador Dalí's unique sleeping technique?

        「サルバドール・ダリのユニークな睡眠技法を試してみませんか」

        → Why don't you try Salvador Dalí's unique sleeping technique?

            「サルバドール・ダリのユニークな睡眠技法を試してみたら」

Your friend: I have a bad headache but we have an exam today. Should I go to school?

You: Why don't you ¹_____?

    You ²_____.

② ①で書いた内容を元にクラスメートと話し合いましょう。

Behind the Scenes   眠りの効用

ヒトの睡眠は、ノンレム睡眠とレム睡眠という質的に異なる二つの睡眠段階に分類されます。ノンレム睡眠とよばれる深い眠りの間に、体内では回復や修復が行われ、レム睡眠中には夢をよく見ます。ノンレム－レム睡眠周期は90分から120分で、朝方になるにしたがってレム睡眠が多くなります。睡眠の効用としてはまずは疲労回復ですが、その他に肥満防止、ストレス解消、記憶の定着などもあげられます。本文に出てきたN1は、ノンレム睡眠中で一番眠りの浅い段階に当たります。

UNIT 2

氷上のチェスという異名をもつほどの戦略とマシンのような精密さがプレーヤーに求められるカーリング競技に、AIを搭載したロボットが登場しました。その名もカーリー。シミュレーションには強いが、現実世界の対応には弱いというこれまでのAIマシンの弱点を克服し、カーリーはプロチームを破ります。

Curly the Curling Robot Can Beat the Pros at Their Own Game

Before You Read

A 日本語の意味に合うように、空所に適切な語を語群から選んで書きましょう。語群には1つ余分なものがあります。

1. 試合では、極わずかな不確定要素のすべてが結果に影響を与える
   all of the subtle (   ) at play impact the outcome

2. 人工知能（AI）を搭載したロボットがプロのカーリングチームと対戦した
   a robot (   ) by AI competed against professional curling teams

3. このロボットはトップランクのチームを相手に健闘した
   the robot gave a top-ranked team a (   ) for their money

4. （それは）車輪を転がし、コンベアベルトを使ってカーリングストーンを回転させる
   it (   ) on wheels and uses a conveyer belt to rotate the curling stone

5. 氷床の組成は一投ごとに変わる
   the composition of the ice sheet changes with each (   )

   | rolls   run   variables   space   throw   powered |

B 下線部の英語の意味として適切な日本語を空所に書きましょう。

1. referred to as "chess on ice"　　　「氷上のチェス」(   )
2. push stones across frozen sheets　　氷床を (   ) ストーンを押し出す
3. knock stones out of central rings　　ストーンを中央の円 (   )
4. the pressure exerted by one's hand　人の手により (   ) 圧力
5. judge uncontrollable environmental conditions (   ) 環境条件を判断する

Reading

Notes

[1] The sport of curling requires such precision and strategy that it's sometimes referred to as "chess on ice." Players push 40-pound stones across frozen sheets, rotating the stones just enough that they "curl," and try to knock opposing teams' stones out of central rings.

[2] Subtle variables at play—tiny, ever-changing bumps in ice, the pressure exerted by one's hand, the smoothness of the stone—all impact the outcome, so much that curling requires machine-like precision from its players.

[3] So, it makes sense that an actual machine might have a shot at winning, if it could learn to strategize on its own. Enter Curly: a robot powered by artificial intelligence (AI) that recently competed against professional South Korean curling teams and won three out of four official matches.

[4] Curly's impressive feat is recounted in an article published this month in *Science Robotics* by researchers Seong-Whan Lee and Dong-Ok Won of Korea University and Klaus-Robert Müller of the Berlin Institute of Technology. The robot gave a top-ranked women's team and a national wheelchair team a run for their money, the authors write, thanks to its "adaptive deep reinforcement learning framework."

[5] Curly actually consists of two robots that communicate with each other: a "skipper" that aims the stone and a "thrower" that pushes it across the ice, reports Brooks Hays for United Press International (UPI). It rolls on wheels and uses a conveyer belt to rotate the curling stone, reports Matt Simon for *Wired* magazine. One camera on Curly's "head" is able to give the robot a view of the field, and another camera just above its front wheels watches the "hogline," or the boundary on the ice where players are required to release the stone.

[6] Researchers designed Curly to assess risk and judge uncontrollable environmental conditions, per UPI. In curling,

bump
平らな表面の突起、隆起

make sense
道理にかなう、当然である
have a shot at winning
勝ち目がある
strategize 戦略を練る
on one's own
自力で、独力で

feat 偉業
recount 詳細を話す

Korea University
高麗大学
Berlin Institute of Technology
ベルリン工科大学

adaptive 適応できる
reinforcement 強化

United Press International
UPI 通信社

Wired ワイアード。テクノロジーが及ぼす影響をテーマにしたアメリカの月刊誌。
hogline ホッグライン

14

the composition of the ice sheet changes with each throw, so
Curly had to learn how to adapt and make corrections on
each subsequent throw.

7 As Devin Coldewey reports for *TechCrunch*, the
achievement is remarkable because Curly is able to make
decisions in real-time as it plays the game.

8 "The game of curling can be considered a good testbed
for studying the interaction between artificial intelligence
systems and the real world," Lee, co-author on the study,
tells UPI. AI machines often perform well in simulations but
struggle to cope in the real world, a problem known as the
"sim-to-real gap," Hays notes.

9 This problem is particularly relevant to curling, because
no two ice sheets are ever the same, reports *Wired*. Each time
a stone is thrown, the ice's bumpy surface will change.
Researchers programmed Curly with physics models that
simulate the ice sheet, and then trained Curly to use its test
throws at the beginning of the match to adjust its models
accordingly.

10 Then, when Curly's camera rises up on its long neck to
look at the field, the researchers programmed the robot to
assess the riskiness of each possible move.

Notes	

testbed　たたき台

sim-to-real gap
シミュレーションと現実世界の
ギャップ

physics model　物理モデル

Extra Notes

l. 16 Science Robotics：アメリカ科学振興協会が発行する学術雑誌『サイエンス』誌のロボット版
l. 38 TechCrunch：主にIT系のベンチャーやWebに関するニュースを配信しているアメリカのニュースサイト

Comprehension Questions

A 記事の内容に一致するものには T（True）、一致しないものには F（False）に丸をつけ、判断の基準になったパラグラフの番号を （ ） に書き込みましょう。ただし、基準とするパラグラフは複数ある場合もあります。

1. Curly is composed of two robots, a "skipper" and a "thrower," which communicate with each other.　　　　　　　　　　　　　　　　　　　T / F （　　　）

2. The physics models researchers used to program Curly cannot simulate the ice sheet.　　　　　　　　　　　　　　　　　　　　　T / F （　　　）

3. Curly can assess risk and judge uncontrollable environmental conditions since it is so designed.　　　　　　　　　　　　　　　　　　　T / F （　　　）

4. The sport of curling requires such precision in targeting the central ring that it's sometimes referred to as "bowling on ice."　　　　　　　　　T / F （　　　）

5. Curly is a robot powered by AI that recently beat professional South Korean curling teams in three out of four games.　　　　　　　　　　T / F （　　　）

B 以下は記事の要約です。適切な語を空所に書き入れ、音声を聞いて答えを確認しましょう。

🎧 DL 04　　💿 CD 1-21

　　　　The sport of curling requires both precision and (**s** 　　　　　　　 ¹). Since subtle (**v** 　　　　　　　 ²) at play such as ever-changing (**b** 　　　　　　　 ³) in ice and the (**s** 　　　　　　　 ⁴) of the stone impact the outcome, (**m** 　　　　　　　 ⁵) -like precision is required from curling players. That's where a robot powered by artificial (**i** 　　　　　　　 ⁶) comes in. This curling robot, Curly, is made of (**t** 　　　　　　　 ⁷) robots communicating with each other, a "skipper" and a "thrower." It rolls on (**w** 　　　　　　　 ⁸) and uses a (**c** 　　　　　　　 ⁹) belt to rotate the curling stone. Curly can assess risk and judge uncontrollable environmental conditions. In particular, it is (**r** 　　　　　　　 ¹⁰) that Curly is able to make (**d** 　　　　　　　 ¹¹) in real-time as it plays the game.

Read Better, Understand More!

句読点（ピリオド、カンマ、コロン、セミコロン、ダッシュ）

音読を行うときに役立つのが句読点（punctuation）です。

カンマは意味、構造、リズム的な区切りを、ピリオドは文の終わりを示します。カンマで息継ぎをし、ピリオドで一拍置くことで、音読がスムーズになります。またダッシュやコロンなどの句読点は、続く文の内容を予告しており、これを理解すると英語が速く正確に読めます。一方、英文を書くときにpunctuationを間違って使用すると意味が変わることもあり注意が必要です。

ダッシュ（—）は、その前の部分をさらに説明し、具体例のリストアップに用います。本文ではダッシュで挟まれた部分がsubtle variablesの内容を示しています。

Subtle variables at play—tiny, ever-changing bumps in ice, the pressure exerted by one's hand, the smoothness of the stone—all impact the outcome...

「試合では、氷にできた小さな絶え間なく変化する突起、手から加わる圧力、ストーンの滑らかさ、といったごくわずかな不確定要素のすべてが結果に影響を与える」

コロン（：）は、その前の部分を説明します。本文ではコロン以下はCurlyの説明になっています。

Enter Curly: a robot powered by artificial intelligence (AI) that recently competed against professional South Korean curling teams...

「カーリーの登場：最近韓国のプロカーリングチームと対戦した、人工知能を搭載したロボット」

セミコロン（；）は、ピリオドで文を2つに分けたくはないが、カンマよりも強く区切りたいときに使われます。例えば次のように使うことができます。

Spin clockwise and the stone will curl right; spin counterclockwise and it'll go left.

「ストーンは右回りに回転させると右に曲がり、左回りに回転させると左に行く」

Exercise

次の空所にダッシュ、コロン、セミコロンの中から適切なものを1つずつ選び書き入れましょう。

1. The sport of curling requires two things (　　　　) precision and strategy.
2. AI machines often perform well in simulations (　　　　) they struggle to cope in the real world, a problem known as the "sim-to-real gap."
3. Curly (　　　　) a robot designed to assess risk and judge uncontrollable environmental conditions, owing to its "adaptive deep reinforcement learning framework."

After You Read

A 会話を聞き、空所を埋めましょう。その後、会話をペアで練習しましょう。

Ava: At last ¹_____ curling as well. The title of today's Smithsonian Magazine article reads "Curly the Curling Robot Can Beat the Pros at Their Own Game."

Ethan: Curling is referred to as "chess on ice," right? ²_____ _____30 years since AI beat humans in chess. Don't you think Curly's appearance is a bit too late?

Ava: Well, curling is ³_____ , which is played on a changeless board. In curling, the ⁴_____ _____ does change with each throw.

Ethan: That means programmed simulations based on physics models alone won't work?

Ava: That's right. What is remarkable about Curly is ⁵_____ _____ , based on the test throws at the beginning of the match.

B 以下の1と2の問題に答えましょう。

『What is ～ about…（…の～なところ）』の～に適当な形容詞を入れることで、さまざまな表現が可能になります。（例）good, bad, wrong, exciting, special, unusualなど

1 上記の説明と以下の例を参考にして、自分の言葉で文章の空所を埋めましょう。

  ex) What is remarkable about Curly is...「カーリーの素晴らしいところは…」

    What is good about living in a dormitory is you don't have to cook dinner by yourself.「寮生活の良いところは、自分で夕食を作らなくても良いことだ」

  What is ¹_____ about living near the university is ²_____ . You can ³_____ .

2 1で書いた内容を元にクラスメートと話し合いましょう。

Behind the Scenes   戦略を要するゲームの世界でプロを破るコンピューター

氷上ならぬ盤上のチェスの世界で、初めて人間を破ったのは Deep Thought（ディープ・ソート）で、1988年にグランドマスターのベント・ラーセンに勝利しました。将棋は、獲得した駒の再利用が可能で手数が多いので「コンピューターが勝つのはチェスより難しい」と言われてきました。しかし 2013 年に、将棋ソフト Ponanza（ポナンザ）が佐藤慎一四段（当時）を破り、将棋の公式戦では初めて、コンピューターが現役プロ棋士に勝ちました。

UNIT

3

ピザが大好き、でも強いアレルギーがあり、イーストで発酵させたピザが食べられないイタリアの材料科学者が発明したのは、イーストを使わずにピザを膨らませる方法でした。ピザ生地をオートクレーブに入れ、ちょうどソーダ水をつくるときのように、高圧のガスにさらすと、生地が膨らみ、おいしいピザが焼けました。

Italian Scientists Create Rising Pizza Dough without Yeast

Before You Read

A 日本語の意味に合うように、空所に適切な語を語群から選んで書きましょう。語群には１つ余分なものがあります。

1. 彼は重度のイーストアレルギーをもっているため、蕁麻疹が出る

   he has a severe yeast allergy that causes him to (　　　　　　　　　　) out in hives

2. イーストに頼って発酵を行い、二酸化炭素の泡を作り出す

   rely on yeast to (　　　　　　　　　　) and produce carbon dioxide bubbles

3. イーストを使わずにこれと同じ気泡の効果を作り出せるだろうかと興味を抱いた

   they were curious if they could produce the same (　　　　　　) effect without yeast

4. 発明は料理中に起こっている事柄への深い理解に基づいている

   invention is (　　　　　　) on a deep knowledge of what's going on while cooking

5. 生地が発酵する際、イーストは風味も与える

   yeast also (　　　　　　　　　　) flavor into the dough as it ferments

   > go　break　bubbly　imparts　ferment　grounded

B 下線部の英語の意味として適切な日本語を空所に書きましょう。

1. a method of <u>leavening</u> pizza dough　　ピザ生地を (　　　　　　　　　) 方法
2. artificially <u>aerate</u> the crust　　クラストに人工的に (　　　　　　)
3. <u>ended up with</u> a set of miniature pizzas　　ミニサイズのピザを (　　　　　　)
4. the <u>lab-puffed</u> crusts　　この (　　　　　　　　) クラスト
5. <u>airborne</u> yeast in our environment　　我々の周りの (　　　　　　　) イースト

Reading

◉ CD 1-23 ～ ◉ CD 1-33

Notes

[1] Ernesto Di Maio can't eat standard pizza. The materials scientist from Naples, Italy, has a severe yeast allergy that causes him to break out in hives. Now, in work published in the journal *Physics of Fluids*, Di Maio and his colleagues
5 have invented a yeast-free method of leavening pizza dough that tastes "exactly like the yeast pizza," he tells *NPR*'s Ari Daniel.

Physics of Fluids
米国物理学協会が毎月発行している流体力学分野の学術誌
NPR 米国公共ラジオ放送

[2] Typical pizza doughs, like most breads, rely on yeast to ferment and produce carbon dioxide bubbles. As the pizza
10 bakes, the air bubbles are cooked into the dough, creating a crust with a fluffy, airy texture. Di Maio and his team were curious if they could produce the same bubbly effect without yeast.

fluffy フワっとした
airy 軽くてフワフワの

[3] "The aim was to try to make the same texture that we
15 love so much in pizza without a chemical agent," says study co-author Rossana Pasquino, a University of Naples chemical engineer, to *Science*'s George Musser.

[4] To artificially aerate the crust, the team placed the dough—a mixture of flour, water, and salt—into an
20 autoclave, a chamber with controlled pressure and temperature settings. They then flooded the golf ball–sized dough with gas at high pressure, similar to carbonating a soda. When they gradually released the pressure and increased the heat inside the chamber, the team watched the
25 dough rise.

autoclave 加圧滅菌器
chamber 閉じられた空間

carbonating
炭酸ガスを入れること

[5] "The invention is grounded on a deep knowledge of what's going on while cooking," Di Maio says to *CNN*'s Kristen Rogers via email. "We had fun in the lab."

[6] Because their autoclave is roughly the size of a toaster
30 oven, the team ended up with a set of miniature pizzas. When they sampled their creation, "it was nice and crusty and soft," Di Maio tells *Science*.

crusty 表面の硬い

[7] Yeast also imparts flavor into the dough as it ferments, which makes some skeptical that the lab-puffed crusts will

skeptical 懐疑的な、疑い深い、疑問をもつ

35 be as tasty as standard yeast-leavened versions.

8 "Yeast does so many things to dough besides fermentation, like the flavors that you find, the complexity of aromas," says Francisco Migoya, head chef at the culinary innovation collective Modernist Cuisine, who wasn't involved

40 in the experiment, to *NPR*. Like creating a sourdough starter, Migoya notes, small amounts of airborne yeast in our environment will find their way into the dough, making a truly yeast-free dough hard to achieve.

9 The researchers say their dough isn't intended for all

45 pizza enthusiasts, but as an alternative for those with dietary restrictions, like Di Maio. The team is optimistic that their aeration technique might improve the texture of gluten-free pizzas, too.

10 "This new technology can drive the development of new

50 products, new dough formulations, and specific recipes for food intolerance, hopefully helping people enjoy healthy and tasty food," Di Maio says in a press release.

11 Following the success of their pint-sized pies, the Italian team plans to use a larger autoclave to produce standard-

55 size pizzas.

Notes
culinary　料理の
sourdough サワードウ、サワー種
Intended for ～向きである、～を対象としている
formulation　処方
food intolerance 食物不耐性
pint-sized　小型の

Extra Notes

l. 17 Science：サイエンス誌。アメリカ科学振興協会によって発行されている学術雑誌　*l. 39* Modernist Cuisine：モダニスト・キュイジーヌ。料理を研究するシェフ、科学者、写真家、編集者、マーケティング専門家などからなるチーム

Comprehension Questions

A 記事の内容に一致するものには T（True）、一致しないものには F（False）に丸をつけ、判断の基準になったパラグラフの番号を（　）に書き込みましょう。ただし、基準とするパラグラフは複数ある場合もあります。

1. By flooding the pizza dough with gas at high pressure, then gradually reducing the pressure and increasing the heat inside the chamber, the researchers made the pizza dough rise.　　　　　　　　　　T / F （　　　　　）

2. Some people doubt if the lab-puffed crusts will be as tasty as standard yeast-leavened versions, since yeast also imparts flavor into the dough as it ferments.
　　　　　　　　　　T / F （　　　　　）

3. This new technology can be useful for developing new products, new dough formulations, and specific recipes for food intolerance.　　　　T / F （　　　　　）

4. Since the Italian team is satisfied with nice and crusty miniature pizzas, they have no plans to use a larger autoclave to produce standard-size pizzas.　　T / F （　　　　　）

5. Di Maio and his colleagues were successful in inventing a yeast-free method of leavening pizza dough, but according to their report, the product did not taste like real yeast pizza.
　　　　　　　　　　T / F （　　　　　）

B 以下は記事の要約です。適切な語を空所に書き入れ、音声を聞いて答えを確認しましょう。

🎧 DL 06　⊙ CD 1-34

　　　A (**m**　　　　　　　^{1}) scientist from Italy and his team have invented a yeast-free method of leavening pizza dough that tastes exactly like yeast pizza. Typical pizza doughs (**r**　　　　　　　^{2}) on yeast to (**f**　　　　　　　^{3}) and produce carbon (**d**　　　　　　　^{4}) bubbles; as the pizza bakes, the air bubbles are cooked into the dough, creating a crust with a fluffy, (**a**　　　　　　　^{5}) texture. To artificially (**a**　　　　　　　^{6}) the crust, the team placed the dough into an (**a**　　　　　　　^{7}), flooded the dough with gas at high pressure, then gradually released the pressure and increased the heat inside the chamber. The created pizza was nice and (**c**　　　　　　　^{8}) and soft. The new technology will hopefully drive the development of new products, new dough formulations, and specific recipes for food intolerance.

Read Better, Understand More!

助動詞

　「AとBが反応してCができる」はA reacts with B to produce C. です。ここには、推量も不確かさも存在していません。しかし、そこに「反応するに違いない」や「反応するはずだ」など、書き手の見方や考えが加わるとき、助動詞が登場します。

1）AはBと反応するに違いない。　　　→ A must react with B.
2）AはBと反応するはずだ。　　　　　→ A can react with B.
3）AはBと反応するだろう。　　　　　→ A would react with B.
4）AはBと反応するかもしれない。　　→ A may (might) react with B.

　ここでwillに注目してみましょう。科学英語でwillは「ほぼ確実に起こる未来のことを示す」ときに使います。本文に登場した例を見てみましょう。

small amounts of airborne yeast in our environment will find their way into the dough, making a truly yeast-free dough hard to achieve.
「我々の周りの空気中を浮遊している少量のイーストが生地の中に入り込むので、真にイーストを含まない生地を作るのは難しい」

　この表現では、空気中にただよっているイーストが生地の中に入り込むのは「ほぼ確実に起こる未来のこと」であり「おそらく～だろう」と推量しているわけではありません。

　またwillは「一般的性質を表す」ときにも使用されます。次の例を見てください。
Gasoline floats on water.　　　　　「ガソリンは水に浮く」
Gasoline will float on water.　　　　「ガソリンは水に浮くものだ」
　willがあることで、「ガソリンには水に浮くという性質がある」というニュアンスが加わります。

Exercise

日本語と同じ意味になるように、空欄に適切な助動詞を入れましょう。

1. この反応は2、3時間続くはずだ。

　　The reaction (　　　　　　　　　　　　) last 2 to 3 hours.

2. その結果は陽性に違いない。

　　This result (　　　　　　　　　　) be positive.

3. 観察から有用な結果を得られるかもしれない。

　　Observations (　　　　　　　　　　　) provide useful results.

After You Read

Ⓐ 会話を聞き、空所を埋めましょう。その後、会話をペアで練習しましょう。

Mark: **1**_____ from milk and homemade jam.

　　　 2_____?

Lisa: It looks **3**_____! But I can't taste it,

　　 unfortunately. I get diarrhea* after drinking milk, since I have lactose** intolerance.

Mark: I didn't know that. What is lactose intolerance? **4**_____

　　 _____?

Lisa: Food intolerance is different from food allergy. In my case, I can't digest lactose. That's

　　 why I don't eat dairy products.

Mark: Hmm. **5**_____ food

　　 intolerance?

Lisa: Yes, food intolerances are common. According to some estimates, they may affect 15 to

　　 20 percent of the population.

Mark: I see. But you appear to be perfectly healthy.

*diarrhea：下痢　　　**lactose：乳糖

Ⓑ 以下の①と②の問題に答えましょう。

① 以下の例を見て、自分の言葉で文章の空所を埋めましょう。

　　ex) You are perfectly healthy.「あなたは健康そのものだ」

　　　　→ You appear to be perfectly healthy.「あなたは健康そのものにみえる」

　　　　A vegan diet is effective against obesity.「ヴィーガンダイエットは肥満に有効だ」

　　　　→ A vegan diet seems to be effective against obesity.「ヴィーガンダイエットは肥満に

　　　　　有効なようだ」

　　1_____ appear to be **2**_____.

　　3_____ seem to be **4**_____.

② ①で書いた内容を元にクラスメートと話し合いましょう。

Behind the Scenes　　食物アレルギー

食物アレルギーは、ある特定の食べ物を食べた後、免疫反応の一つとして蕁麻疹、下痢、咳などのアレルギー反応があらわれる疾患です。これは体から異物を排出するためのメカニズムと言えます。一方、食物不耐症とは、特定の食物を消化する酵素をもたない疾患です。例えば乳糖不耐症の人は、乳糖を消化する酵素を持たないため、牛乳を飲むと下痢をしますが、これはアレルギーではなく食物不耐症なのです。

UNIT 4

増える一方のプラスチック廃棄物との戦いは新たな局面を迎えています。これまでのリサイクルでは、プラごみは衣料品や再生プラスチック製品へと生まれ変わっていました。ところが、このたび研究者たちは、遺伝子組み換えを行った大腸菌を使い、プラごみから何とバニラエッセンスを作り出すことに成功したのです。

Plastic Waste Can Be Transformed into Vanilla Flavoring

Before You Read

A 日本語の意味に合うように、空所に適切な語を語群から選んで書きましょう。語群には1つ余分なものがあります。

1. 科学者は世界的危機と戦う革新的なアプローチを発見した

scientists found an ( ) approach to combat the global crisis

2. バニラビーンズ抽出物の主成分である、バニリン

vanillin, the primary component of vanilla bean ( )

3. バニラの市場価格は7億2450万ドルに達すると予測される

vanilla has a market value ( ) to reach $724.5 million

4. バニリンはバニラにその特徴的な甘い香りを与える

vanillin gives vanilla its signature sweet ( )

5. 世界のバニラの85%は化石燃料から合成されている

eighty-five percent of the world's vanilla is ( ) from fossil fuels

synthesized　elemental　innovative　extract　aroma　predicted

B 下線部の英語の意味として適切な日本語を空所に書きましょう。

1. convert plastic into vanilla flavoring　プラスチックをバニラエッセンスに（　　　）る

2. genetically engineered bacteria　遺伝子組み換えされた（　　　）

3. valuable industrial chemical　貴重な工業（　　　）

4. vanillin is produced artificially　バニリンは（　　　）に製造される

5. enzymes can break down plastic bottles　（　　　）はペットボトルを分解できる

Reading

	Notes

1 Scientists have found an innovative approach to combat the global plastic waste crisis and make something sweeter in the process.

2 To meet the demands for vanillin, the primary
5 component of vanilla bean extract, and reduce plastic waste, researchers are converting plastic into vanilla flavoring using genetically engineered bacteria, according to a new study published in *Green Chemistry*. This study marks the first time researchers brewed up a "valuable" chemical
10 compound from plastic waste, reports Damian Carrington for *The Guardian*.

3 "This is the first example of using a biological system to upcycle plastic waste into a valuable industrial chemical and this has very exciting implications for the circular economy,"
15 study author Joanna Sadler, a biochemist at the University of Edinburgh, says in a statement.

4 As a lucrative spice, vanilla has a market value predicted to reach $724.5 million by 2025 as demand rapidly increases, reports Kate Ng for *The Independent*.

20 **5** Vanillin is what gives vanilla its signature sweet aroma and potent flavor. It is found in various items, including dairy products, soda, and cosmetics, reports Asha C. Gilbert for *USA Today*. Normally, the chemical compound is distilled from the extract of vanilla beans; however, it can also be
25 made synthetically. Eighty-five percent of the world's vanilla is synthesized from fossil fuels in a two-step process, per *The Independent*. Vanillin is produced artificially to meet demands that the vanilla bean supply can't meet, reports Yasemin Saplakoglu for *Live Science*.

30 **6** Currently, single-use plastics lose 95 percent of their value after use, causing a $110 billion loss to global markets every year, *USA Today* reports. For every one million plastic bottles sold each minute globally, only 14 percent is recycled, reports *The Guardian*.

Notes:

brew 醸造する

upcycle
付加価値の高いものに作り替えること。創造的再利用。
implication 意味あい
circular economy
循環型経済
lucrative 収益の大きい

potent 強力な、強い

distill 蒸留する

Live Science
p. 8 *l*. 7参照

7 Previous studies found enzymes could break down plastic bottles made from polyethylene terephthalate (PET) into terephthalic acid (TA). Building on this finding, researchers used a modified version of the bacteria *Escherichia coli* to convert the acid into vanillin. The team mixed a broth containing the engineered *E. coli* and TA at a temperature of 98.6 degrees Fahrenheit for a day, reports *The Guardian*. The bacteria converted 79 percent of the TA into vanillin. Because both chemical compounds are similar, the microbes could easily transform the acid into vanillin. The bacteria only need to make a few changes to the number of hydrogen and oxygen atoms bonded to the acid's carbon ring, *Live Science* reports.

plastic waste

Terephthalic acid
plastic monomer

engineered
E. coli

Vanillin
value-added product

8 "Using microbes to turn waste plastics, which are harmful to the environment, into an important commodity and platform molecule with broad applications in cosmetics and food is a beautiful demonstration of green chemistry," Ellis Crawford, a medicinal chemist and editor at the journal Royal Society of Chemistry, says in a statement.

9 For future studies, the researchers are looking into how they can use the bacteria to increase the amount of TA converted into vanillin and scale the process so more extensive amounts of plastic can be converted at a time, reports *The Guardian*.

Notes

polyethylene terephthalate
ポリエチレンテレフタレート
terephthalic acid
テレフタル酸
build on
〜に基づいてことを進める
Escherichia coli　大腸菌
broth　培養液

microbe　微生物、細菌

carbon ring　炭素環

platform molecule
プラットフォーム分子

medicinal chemist
医薬品化学者
Royal Society of Chemistry
英国王立化学会

scale　拡大する

Extra Notes

l. 8 Green Chemistry：英国王立化学会が発行しているグリーンケミストリー（物質を設計、合成、応用するときに有害物をなるべく使わない、出さない化学）分野の学術誌。

Comprehension Questions

A 記事の内容に一致するものには T (True)、一致しないものには F (False) に丸をつけ、判断の基準になったパラグラフの番号を（ ）に書き込みましょう。ただし、基準となるパラグラフは複数ある場合もあります。

1. Currently 85 percent of the world's production of vanillin, which is responsible for the characteristic taste and smell of vanilla, is distilled from the extract of vanilla beans, according to *The Independent*.　　**T / F** （　　　）

2. Next, the scientists will further study the conditions for the bacteria to increase the conversion rate and work on scaling up the process to convert larger amounts of plastic.　　**T / F** （　　　）

3. Plastic bottles have long been converted into vanilla flavoring using genetically engineered bacteria from waste plastic.　　**T / F** （　　　）

4. The enzymes which can break down plastic bottles into terephthalic acid (TA) have already been found by other researchers.　　**T / F** （　　　）

5. Vanillin is an expensive substance and demand for it is growing rapidly, with a market size projected to be worth US$724.5 million by 2025.　　**T / F** （　　　）

B 以下は記事の要約です。適切な語を空所に書き入れ、音声を聞いて答えを確認しましょう。

🎧 DL 08　　⊙ CD 1-45

　　Scientists have found an (**i**　　　　　 ¹) approach to combat the global plastic waste crisis: they are converting plastic into vanilla flavoring using genetically engineered bacteria. Vanillin is the primary (**c**　　　　　 ²) of vanilla bean extract, and gives vanilla its signature sweet (**a**　　　　　 ³) and potent flavor. It is contained in various items, including dairy products, soda, and cosmetics, and is currently produced (**a**　　　　　 ⁴) to meet demands that the vanilla bean supply can't meet. It was already found that some (**e**　　　　　 ⁵) could break down plastic bottles made from polyethylene terephthalate (**P**　　　　　 ⁶) into terephthalic acid. Building on this (**f**　　　　　 ⁷), researchers used a modified bacteria, *Escherichia coli*, to (**c**　　　　　 ⁸) the acid into vanillin. The team mixed a (**b**　　　　　 ⁹) containing the engineered *E. coli* and the acid at a temperature of 98.6 degrees Fahrenheit for a day, and the microbes could easily (**t**　　　　　 ¹⁰) the acid into vanillin. This must be a beautiful (**d**　　　　　 ¹¹) of green chemistry.

Read Better, Understand More!

抽象名詞が普通名詞になるとき

温度や圧力などの抽象名詞には不定冠詞はつきません。次の例を見てみましょう。

a graph with temperature on the horizontal axis and pressure on the vertical axis
「温度を横軸に、圧力を縦軸にとったグラフ」

ここではtemperatureもpressureもそれぞれ温度と圧力という抽象的な概念を表す抽象名詞なので無冠詞になっています。
ところで、本文では下記のようにtemperatureに不定冠詞のaがついていました。

The team mixed a broth containing the engineered *E.coli* and TA at a temperature of 98.6 degrees Fahrenheit... 「このチームは遺伝子組み換えを行った大腸菌とTAを含んだ培養液を華氏98.6度で混合した」

その理由はここではtemperatureが温度という概念を表しているのではなく、℉を単位とした一つの数値で示される温度を表しているからなのです。ある一つの数値で示される温度はa temperatureとなり、複数の数値で示される場合はtemperaturesとなります。
次の例を見てください。

Some precipitates lose water readily in an oven at temperatures between 110℃ and 130℃. 「沈殿の中には乾燥器中、110℃から130℃の温度で簡単に脱水するものもある」

この場合temperaturesは110℃から130℃の間にある複数の温度の値（例えば110℃, 111℃, 113.5℃など）を指しているのです。

Exercise

日本語と同じ意味になるように、英文の中のtemperatureを適切な形に変え、必要に応じて冠詞を書き加えましょう。

1. 鉛は328℃で融ける。

Lead melts at *temperature* of 328℃.

2. この作物は低温に弱い。

This crop is vulnerable to low *temperature*.

3. わずかな温度の変化が環境に大きな変化を引き起こす。

Small changes in *temperature* cause enormous changes in the environment.

After You Read

DL 09 CD 1-46

A 会話を聞き、空所を埋めましょう。その後、会話をペアで練習しましょう。

Paul: Your morning cup of coffee is brewed!

Marie: Thanks. [1]_____, you know what, now scientists have brewed vanilla flavoring from plastic waste.

Paul: Wait a minute! [2]_____ "have brewed vanilla flavoring from plastic waste?"

Marie: Just like brewing beer, they mixed a broth containing special bacteria and terephthalic acid (TA) obtained from plastic waste at a certain temperature for a day and obtained vanillin, [3]_____.

Paul: I find it amazing! I thought recycling plastic waste only [4]_____ _____. It seems like bacteria have unknown powers.

Marie: Vanillin is used not only in ice cream but also in cosmetics and home fragrances. It is a revolutionary invention [5]_____ _____.

B 以下の①と②の問題に答えましょう。

① 以下の例を見て、自分の言葉で文章の空所を埋めましょう。

ex) It is amazing.「それは素晴らしい」

　　→ I find it amazing.「私はそれが素晴らしいと思う」

I found this article [1]_____. Until now, I thought that plastic waste [2]_____. Maybe in the future, I hope [3]_____ to solve the ever-growing plastic waste problem.

② ①で書いた内容を元にクラスメートと話し合いましょう。

Behind the Scenes　　大腸菌を活用する

本文に登場したgenetically engineered *Escherichia coli*とは、遺伝子組み換えにより触媒としての機能を与えられた大腸菌のことです。増殖速度が速く，遺伝子改変が容易な大腸菌は現在医薬品の合成でも大活躍しています。1920年代に動物の膵臓から抽出されていたインスリンは非常に高価で、アレルギーなどの副作用もありましたが、1980年代にヒトインスリン遺伝子を導入した大腸菌による大量生産が可能となり、糖尿病患者の寿命が飛躍的に伸びました。

地球温暖化の原因となる二酸化炭素やメタンガスは一般家庭のガスコンロからも放出されています。さらにコンロの栓を閉めていても、そこから実はガスが漏れ出ており、これらのガスは喘息や咳の原因となっていることが、アメリカで行われたリサーチの結果判明しました。

UNIT

5

Gas Stoves Are Worse for Climate and Health than Previously Thought

Before You Read

A 日本語の意味に合うように、空所に適切な語を語群から選んで書きましょう。語群には1つ余分なものがあります。

1. ガスコンロがそこにあるだけで、メタンの放出量を増やしている

the ( ) existence of the stoves is what's driving those methane emissions

2. 彼らはガスで調理をしており、それに加えて暖房器具や温水器からの暴露もある

they cook with gas, and get additional exposure from ( ) and water heaters

3. 喘息や咳を引き起こし、呼吸器感染症にかかりやすくさせる

( ) asthma, coughing, and increase susceptibility to respiratory infections

4. ガスの濃度を求めるために光の波長を測定する

measure ( ) of light to determine the concentration of gases

5. 吸い込むと深刻な健康被害を引き起こすガス

gases that pose serious health risks when ( )

---

trigger   inhaled   wavelengths   mere   exhaled   space

B 下線部の英語の意味として適切な日本語を空所に書きましょう。

1. half a million <u>gas-powered cars</u>　　　　　50万台の（ ）

2. these natural gas-burning <u>appliances</u>　　　天然ガス燃焼（ ）

3. creates nitrogen dioxide as a <u>byproduct</u>　　二酸化窒素を（ ）として生成する

4. gas stoves imperil <u>the planet</u>　　　　　　ガスコンロは（ ）危険にさらす

5. a huge <u>contributor</u> to planetary warming　地球温暖化に大きく（ ）

CD 1-47 ～ CD 1-54

Notes

[1] If you live in one of the 40 million American households with a gas stove, it could be leaking even when it's turned off.

[2] According to a new study from Stanford scientists, many stoves are constantly emitting gases that can warm the planet and pose serious health risks when inhaled. The research, which appeared in the journal *Environmental Science & Technology*, found methane emissions from gas stoves across the United States are roughly equivalent to the carbon dioxide released by half a million gas-powered cars in a year.

[3] "The mere existence of the stoves is really what's driving those methane emissions," says study author Eric Lebel, a research scientist with PSE Healthy Energy, to Danielle Renwick for *Nexus Media News*. "We found that over three-quarters of the methane emissions from stoves are emitted while the stove is off. So these little tiny leaks from the stoves, they really do add up."

[4] While leaky natural gas pipelines have been studied extensively, scientists know less about the climate and health impacts of gas-burning stoves. More than a third of Americans cook with gas, and some get additional exposure from space and water heaters. All of these natural gas-burning appliances can emit gases that can trigger asthma, coughing, and potentially increase susceptibility to respiratory infections.

[5] To gauge the impact of these emissions, researchers measured three key gases from stoves in 53 homes across seven California counties. The team chose two gases—methane and carbon dioxide—because of their contribution to climate change, and selected nitrogen oxides because of their known risk to human health. The scientists set up plastic partitions between the kitchens and other rooms and used instruments that measure wavelengths of light to determine the concentration of certain gases.

Environmental Science & Technology
米国化学会が隔週で発行している学術誌

PSE Healthy Energy
米国カリフォルニアの非営利研究機関
Nexus Media News
気候変動に関する記事を発信する非営利のニュースサービス
add up　合計する、増やす
leaky　漏れがある

gauge　正確に測定する、評価する

nitrogen oxides　窒素酸化物

partition　仕切り

35　**6** To their surprise, they found that more than three-quarters of the methane emissions happened when both old and new gas stoves were turned off.

　　7 The most significant health risks happen when the stove is lit, the authors note, because the process creates nitrogen
40　dioxide as a byproduct. Increasing airflow by using a range hood can help reduce the personal health risk of natural gas-burning appliances, but most individuals report rarely using their ventilation system.

　　8 In addition to health risks, natural gas burning stoves
45　also imperil the planet by releasing methane. While carbon dioxide gets the most attention in conversations about climate change, methane is a huge contributor to planetary warming. Following carbon dioxide, methane is the second most abundant greenhouse gas that humans have pumped
50　into the atmosphere, accounting for about 20 percent of global emissions. Although methane dissipates more quickly than carbon dioxide, it is especially concerning because of its heat-trapping power, which is more than 25 times as potent as carbon dioxide. The team estimated that stoves emit
55　between 0.8 and 1.3 percent of the natural gas they consume as unburned methane.

airflow　空気の流れ

ventilation　換気

abundant　豊富な

account for
〜の割合を占める
dissipate　消える、消散する

heat-trapping power
熱を閉じ込める力
potent　p. 26 *l*. 21 参照

Comprehension Questions

A 記事の内容に一致するものには T(True)、一致しないものには F(False)に丸をつけ、判断の基準になったパラグラフの番号を（ ）に書き込みましょう。ただし、基準とするパラグラフは複数ある場合もあります。

1. The most significant health risks happen when the stove is lit and emits nitrogen dioxide during the combustion process. 　　 T / F （　　　　）

2. One out of three Americans cook with gas, and to add to that, some people use space and water heaters. 　　 T / F （　　　　）

3. Carbon dioxide is the most abundant greenhouse gas, and methane is the second most abundant greenhouse gas that we emit into the atmosphere. 　　 T / F （　　　　）

4. Researchers chose three gases for measurement, namely, methane, carbon monoxide and nitrogen oxides. 　　 T / F （　　　　）

5. Gas stoves do not emit methane while the stove is off. 　　 T / F （　　　　）

B 以下は記事の要約です。適切な語を空所に書き入れ、音声を聞いて答えを確認しましょう。

🎧 DL 10 　⊙ CD 1-55

　　Many stoves are (**c**　　　　　　　 [1]) emitting gases that can warm the planet and (**p**　　　　　　 [2]) serious health risks when (**i**　　　　　　 [3]). Over three-quarters of the methane emissions from stoves are emitted while the stove is off. More than a (**t**　　　　　　 [4]) of Americans cook with gas, and get additional exposure from space and water heaters. These natural gas-burning appliances emit gases that can trigger (**a**　　　　　　 [5]), coughing, and increase (**s**　　　　　　 [6]) to respiratory (**i**　　　　　　 [7]). The most significant health risks happen when the stove is lit, because the process creates toxic nitrogen dioxide as a (**b**　　　　　　 [8]). Increasing (**a**　　　　　　 [9]) by using a range (**h**　　　　　 [10]) can help reduce the personal health risk of natural gas-burning appliances, but most individuals rarely use their (**v**　　　　　 [11]) system.

Read Better, Understand More!

物質名詞が普通名詞になるとき

このunitではガスがテーマとなっており、文章中にgasという単語が何度も登場しました。さて、このgasは物質名詞でしょうか？　それとも普通名詞なのでしょうか？

gasが、その具体的な成分について触れられず、単に燃料用のガスの意味で用いられるときは、物質名詞になります。本文で言うと次の例が該当します。

More than a third of Americans cook with gas.
「アメリカ人の３分の１以上がガスで調理をしている」

ところで、一口にガスと言っても、いろいろな種類があります。例えば、ここではメタン、二酸化炭素、窒素酸化物などが登場しました。それら一つ一つの種類について考えるとき、gasは普通名詞になります。メタンガスや二酸化炭素ガスといった、具体的な一つのガスはa gas、それらをまとめるとgasesと表現されるのです。

それでは、次の３つの文のgasesがそれぞれ何を指すのか見てみましょう。

many stoves are constantly emitting gases　　　　→放出されている複数の種類のガスを指す
「多くのガスコンロは常に（何種類かの）ガスを放出している」
researchers measured three key gases　　　　　→メタン、二酸化炭素、窒素酸化物を指す
「研究者は３種類の主要なガスの測定を行った」
concentration of certain gases　　　　　　　　→メタン、二酸化炭素、窒素酸化物を指す
「特定のガスの濃度」

Exercise

日本語と同じ意味になるように、空所に必要な冠詞を書きましょう。冠詞が必要ないときには×を書きましょう。

1. 紅茶に砂糖を入れますか？

Do you put (　　　　　　　) sugar in tea?

2. ブドウ糖は自然界に豊富に存在する単糖です。

Glucose is (　　　　　　) monosaccharide abundant in nature.

3. 善玉脂肪と悪玉脂肪の違いは何ですか？

What is the difference between (　　　　　　) good fat and (　　　　　) bad fat?

After You Read

A 会話を聞き、空所を埋めましょう。その後、会話をペアで練習しましょう。

Jacob: Stoves emit methane, carbon dioxide and other gases while they are off. We should switch to all-electric **1**_____

_____ , according to the morning news.

Mia: But electric stoves are more expensive than gas stoves. That will **2**_____

_____ .

Jacob: Well, those gases you inhale without noticing can trigger asthma, coughing, and potentially **3**_____

_____ . That's more important than a small sum of money.

Mia: Absolutely.

Jacob: Since they are greenhouse gases, electric stoves are **4**_____

_____ .

Mia: Wait a minute. Electricity **5**_____ after all.

B 以下の1と2の問題に答えましょう。

1 以下の例を見て、自分の言葉で文章の空所を埋めましょう。

ex) *A:* That's more important than a small sum of money.「それはわずかな金より重要だ」
　　B: Absolutely.「もちろんよ」／ I see.「なるほど」／ Really?「本当?」／ Exactly.「その
　　通り」／ I think so, too.「私もそう思う」／ Certainly.「確かに」／ I agree.「同感だよ」
Your friend: The article in today's reading section **1**_____

_____ .

You: **2**_____ . I was very surprised to know **3**_____

_____ .

2 1で書いた内容を元にクラスメートと話し合いましょう。

Behind the Scenes　　窒素酸化物 (NOx)

窒素酸化物とは窒素 (N) と酸素 (O) が結合してできる物質の総称で、生成過程の違いにより次の2つに分類されます。一つはfuel NOx とよばれ、燃料が燃えるときに、含まれている窒素が、大気中の酸素と結合して生成されるもの。もう一つはthermal NOx と呼ばれ、高温の燃焼プロセス中、空気中に含まれている窒素と酸素が反応して生成されるものです。窒素酸化物は大気汚染防止法で「ばい煙」に指定されている代表的な大気汚染物質です。

UNIT 6

マッシュルームの菌糸から、本物そっくりのヴィーガンレザー（動物の皮を使わない代替レザー）が誕生しました。環境に優しい高級皮革はすでにエルメスのバッグやアディダスのシューズなどの製品として登場しています。動物愛護、地球温暖化の観点から、皮革を動物に頼るのではなく、サボテンやパイナップルなどの植物から作り出す技術も開発されました。

" This Mushroom-Based Leather Could Be the Next Sustainable Fashion Material "

Before You Read

A 日本語の意味に合うように、空所に適切な語を語群から選んで書きましょう。語群には１つ余分なものがあります。

1. それらは互いに密に絡み合い、最終的には硬い材料を形成する

they become densely (   ), eventually forming a tough material

2. 菌糸体が天然に形成する圧縮された固体の発泡体から作られる

made from a (   ) solid foam that mycelium forms naturally

3. トレーはデザイナーの厳密な仕様に合わせて設計できる

trays can be designed to fit a designer's exact (   )

4. 気候危機や畜産農業への解決策を考え出そうとする

try to (   ) up with solutions for the climate crisis and animal agriculture

5. 牛革の製造は、より大きな破壊を環境にもたらす

manufacturing bovine leather (   ) more havoc on the environment

> specifications compressed come extract intertwined wreaks

B 下線部の英語の意味として適切な日本語を空所に書きましょう。

1. vegan leather derived from <u>fungi</u>　（   ）から得られたヴィーガンレザー

2. processed using <u>chromium-free</u> chemistry　（   ）薬品で処理された

3. <u>jumped on</u> the eco-friendly bandwagon　エコフレンドリーという時流に（   ）

4. buy something, use it, and <u>throw it away</u>　買い、使い、そして（   ）

5. a soft material derived from <u>cactuses</u>　（   ）から作られた柔らかい材料

Reading

Notes

1 Plant-based leathers have the potential to revolutionize the fashion industry. Now, MycoWorks, a California-based biotech company, has created a new eco-friendly, vegan leather derived from fungi. The leather derived from
5 mycelium—threads from the root structure of mushrooms—is a material that imitates the look and feel of animal-based leather, reports Jess Cartner-Morley for *The Guardian*.

2 While the material is mushroom-based, MycoWorks creates its rigid, patented material using engineered
10 mycelium cells. As the cells grow into 3-D structures, they become densely intertwined, eventually forming a tough material, dubbed Fine Mycelium, which has the strength, durability, and performance of traditional leather, according to the MycoWorks website. The result differs from other
15 types of vegan leather made with mushrooms. Most mushroom leather is made from a compressed solid foam that mycelium forms naturally, but without engineering, it lacks the same look and feel as other animal and synthetic leathers.

20 **3** Fine Mycelium can be grown in trays in a short amount of time. These trays can be designed to fit a designer's exact specifications, eliminating any waste from excess scraps, *The Guardian* reports. After the Fine Mycelium is harvested, it is tanned and finished to look and feel like animal leather's
25 unique grain. The result is the product MycoWorks calls Reishi, a leather that is processed using chromium-free chemistry, a chemical found in tannery wastewater, reports Frances Solá-Santiago for *Refinery29*.

4 The vegan leather has already made a high fashion
30 debut. In March 2021, luxury fashion brand Hermés debuted their Victoria bag, which featured MycoWork's Fine Mycelium material, reports Olivia Rosane for *EcoWatch*. Other companies, including Adidas with their Mylo-made Stan Smith shoes and Lululemon with their mushroom-

Notes

revolutionize 革命を起こす、大改革をもたらす

vegan leather 動物由来のものを使用しない人工皮革

mycelium 菌糸体。菌類を構成する細い糸状のものを菌糸といい、その集合体のこと。
root structure 基本構造

dub （ニックネームを）つける
durability 耐久性

scrap くず

tan （皮を）なめす
grain （皮革の）しぼ

tannery 皮なめし工場
wastewater 廃水
Refinery29 米国の若い女性向けデジタルメディア
high fashion 高級ファッション
debut （新商品などを）初めて市場に投入する
feature （～）の特色となる、特徴づける
EcoWatch 環境ニュースを提供するニュースサイト

38

based yoga products, have also jumped on the eco-friendly
bandwagon, per *Refinery29*.

5 The use of plant-based leather comes during a time when
scientists and innovators are trying to come up with
solutions for the climate crisis and animal agriculture.
Manufacturing bovine leather wreaks more havoc on the
environment than any other type of fabric—even plastic-
based leathers—because of deforestation and methane
emissions connected to animals raised for leather and meat,
The Guardian reports. Livestock alone make up nearly 15
percent of the globe's greenhouse gas emissions, *EcoWatch*
reports.

6 Other plant-based leathers have already been in the
works. Material companies Ananas Anam created a natural
textile called Piñatex from waste pineapple leaf fiber, and
Adriano Di Marti invented Deserttex, a soft leather-like
material derived from cactuses that can be used in the
fashion and furniture industries.

7 "We have been trained as consumers to think in terms of
a straight line whereby we buy something, use it, and throw
it away. Fungi can inform thinking about fashion on lots of
levels. This is about material innovation, but it's also about
the culture of making endless new things, and what we can
learn from thinking in terms of nature and of cycles instead,"
says biologist Merlin Sheldrake, author of *Entangled Lives*:
*How Fungi Make Our Worlds, Change Our Minds, and Shape
Our Futures*, to *The Guardian*.

Notes

deforestation　森林破壊

livestock　家畜、家畜類

in the works　進行中

textile　繊維

innovation　革新、刷新

Extra Notes

l. 12 Fine Mycelium：ファイン・マイセリウム、菌糸体からレザーのような素材を作る技術、それによって作られた素材

Comprehension Questions

A 記事の内容に一致するものには T(True)、一致しないものには F(False)に丸をつけ、判断の基準になったパラグラフの番号を（　）に書き込みましょう。ただし、基準とするパラグラフは複数ある場合もあります。

1. Fine Mycelium is tanned and finished with a chemical which does not contain chromium to produce a leather named Reishi.　　　　　T / F （　　　　）

2. Biologist Merlin Sheldrake criticizes the material innovation, and the way in which the leather is produced from fungi.　　　　　T / F （　　　　）

3. The leather produced by MycoWorks is derived from mycelium but imitates the look and feel of animal-based leather.　　　　　T / F （　　　　）

4. People are now trying to produce plant-based leathers from such material as waste pineapple leaf fiber and cactuses.　　　　　T / F （　　　　）

5. Vegan leather derived from mushrooms has been used for fashion products including Adidas Stan Smith shoes and Hermés bags.　　　　　T / F （　　　　）

B 以下は記事の要約です。適切な語を空所に書き入れ、音声を聞いて答えを確認しましょう。

🎧 DL 12　⊙ CD 1-64

MycoWorks, a California-based (**b**　　　　　[1]) company, has created a new eco-friendly, (**v**　　　　　[2]) leather derived from (**f**　　　　　[3]). As mycelium grows into a 3-D (**s**　　　　　[4]), it becomes densely (**i**　　　　　[5]), eventually forming a tough material, which has the strength, (**d**　　　　　[6]), and performance of (**t**　　　　　[7]) leather. After it is harvested, it is (**t**　　　　　[8]) and finished to look and feel like animal leather's unique (**g**　　　　　[9]). The vegan leather has already been used by a (**l**　　　　　[10]) fashion brand, Hermés.

Read Better, Understand More!

前置詞 1

このUnitの本文中、実に約60ものワードが前置詞（about, during, for, from, in, into, of, on, to, with, without）でした。前置詞は名詞の前に置かれ、その前後の単語の関係を規定するという役割を持ちます。

aboutもonも「〜について」という意味を持ちますが、使い方には多少差があります。aboutは以下のように口頭発表など（話し言葉）で使われることが多く、

Today I will talk about ~ 「本日は〜についてお話しします」

一方、onは以下のように論文など（書き言葉で）使われることが多いのです。

A study on ~ 「〜に関する研究」

duringとforは共に「〜の間に」という意味を持ちますが、以下のように使い分けます。duringのあとには時期を表す名詞が、forのあとには数値が来ます。

during a time when scientists ~ 「科学者が〜の時期に」
for 3 hours 「3時間の間」

fromは「〜から」とスタート地点を示しますが、それに対しto は「〜へ」とゴールを示します。

from 10 am to 5 pm 「午前10時から午後5時まで」
from Paris to Tokyo 「パリから東京へ」

場所を示す前置詞には、in「〜の中に」とon「〜の上に（接して）」があります。これに方向を示す前置詞 to が加わると、into「〜の中へ」とonto「〜の上へ」という新しい前置詞ができあがります。inとintoは以下のように使い分けることができます。

Add water to the powder in a beaker. 「ビーカーの中の粉末に水を加える」
Pour water into a beaker. 「ビーカーの中へ水を注ぎ入れる」

Exercise

日本語と同じ意味になるように、空欄に適切な前置詞を入れなさい。

1. その溶液を30℃で1時間加熱した。
   The solution was heated (　　　　　) 30℃ (　　　　　) 1 hour.
2. 混合物を10℃まで氷で冷却した。
   The mixture was cooled (　　　　　) 10℃ with ice.
3. 点Pは線分AB上にある。
   Point P is (　　　　　) line segment AB.

After You Read

A 会話を聞き、空所を埋めましょう。その後、会話をペアで練習しましょう。

Paul: Hey! Did you buy a new bag? It's beautiful.

Jane: This is a new Hermés model. Can you **1**_____?

Paul: It's made of calf leather*, isn't it?

Jane: To tell you the truth, this is made of **2**_____
_____.

Paul: Wow, I can hardly believe that is made from mushrooms.

Jane: Not only mushrooms, but also many other plants **3**_____
_____ have been used recently to produce plant-based leathers.
They can provide solutions for the climate crisis and animal agriculture. In addition,
mushroom leather **4**_____ to fit exact specifications. So
designers have more freedom!

Paul: Well, how about the price?

Jane: It is rather expensive, but I hope the price will go down **5**_____
_____.

*calf leather：生後半年以内の子牛の皮をなめした、最高級の牛革

B 以下の1と2の問題に答えましょう。

1 以下の例を見て、自分の言葉で文章の空所を埋めましょう。

ex) How about (①the price/②going shopping/③we have lunch together)?
　　「(①値段／②買い物に行くの／③お昼を一緒に食べるの) はどう？」

Your friend: We will finish our exams on Friday, and finally summer vacation starts.
　　Let's do something together. Do you have any good ideas?

You: How about **1**_____ together? We can enjoy
2_____ ... I'm sure you will like it.

2 1で書いた内容を元にクラスメートと話し合いましょう。

Behind the Scenes　　なめし (tanning)

そのままでは腐敗してしまう動物の皮 (原皮) を加工して、素材として使える状態 (革) に
することをなめす (tan) といい、その工場がtanneryです。クロム (chromium) なめしは短
期間でなめすことが可能なうえ、加工をしやすいという利点があり、現在の主流です。一
方古くから行われていた手法がタンニンなめしで、ミモザの樹皮などから抽出したタンニ
ン (tannin) を使うものです。この手法で仕上げた革は通称「ヌメ革」とよばれています。

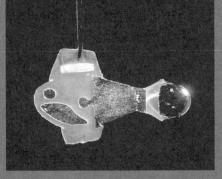

バイオハイブリッド魚は心筋細胞
が収縮する力を利用して、尾びれ
を左右に振り水の中を泳ぎます。
これは、ヒトの心臓の細胞を使っ
た人工心臓の実現に向けての第一
歩。ブタの心臓や、合成物質から
作られる人工心臓を移植するのと
比べ、患者自身の細胞から作られ
る人工心臓移植には予期せぬ恩恵
が得られる可能性があるのです。

UNIT

7

Scientists Build an Artificial Fish that Swims on Its Own Using Human Heart Cells

Before You Read

A 日本語の意味に合うように、空所に適切な語を語群から選んで書きましょう。語群には 1 つ余分なものがあります。

1. 心臓の細胞の収縮を利用し、自力で泳ぎ回る魚を設計した
engineered fish using the (   ) of heart cells to swim autonomously

2. 紙とゼラチンと心筋組織、そしてプラスチックのヒレを用いてこの魚を作り上げた
built the fish using paper, gelatin, cardiac muscle tissue, and a plastic (   )

3. 筋肉ポンプの基本的な法則を理解する
understand the fundamental laws of (   ) pumps

4. 着想をえるべく海洋生物に目を向けた
began looking at marine (   ) for inspiration

5. 遺伝子改変したブタの心臓の移植の方がより可能性が高い
the (   ) of genetically altered pig hearts is more promising

> muscular contractions tail transplantation fin organisms

B 下線部の英語の意味として適切な日本語を空所に書きましょう。

1. improve the development of artificial hearts　人工心臓の（   ）を改善する

2. contractions propelled the fish through the water　収縮により魚は水の中を（   ）

3. ultimately, build a heart for a sick kid　（   ）病児のための心臓を作る

4. it is equivalent to 38 million beats　それは3800万回の（   ）に相当する

5. frustrated by the state of heart therapeutics　（   ）の現状に苛立つ

43

Reading

Notes

1 Harvard scientists have engineered a school of fish that uses the contractions of human heart cells to swim autonomously. Researchers say the experiment could advance pacemaker technology and improve the development of

5　artificial hearts for humans, writes *CNET's* Monisha Ravisetti. The team published their results in the journal *Science*.

CNET
IT分野の情報を提供する米メディアサイト
Science
p. 21 Extra Notes 参照

2 Researchers built the fish using paper, gelatin, two layers of cardiac muscle tissue—one on the left side and one

10　on the right—and a plastic fin, per the study. Muscle contractions propelled the fish through the water. A contraction on one side caused the muscle on the other side to stretch. The stretching then triggered those cells to contract, which moved the tail from side to side and allowed it to swim

15　on its own. The muscle cells were derived from human stem cells, the authors write in the paper. They also engineered an autonomous pacing node, which acted like a pacemaker by controlling the rhythm and frequency of the contractions, per a statement.

move ~ from side to side
～を左右に動かす
on one's own
p. 14 *l*. 11 参照

autonomous　自律性の
pacing　ペーシング
node　ノード、結節

20　**3** "It's a training exercise," Kit Parker, a professor of bioengineering and applied physics at Harvard and senior author of the paper, tells *NPR's* Jon Hamilton. "Ultimately, I want to build a heart for a sick kid."

applied physics
応用物理学
senior author　上席著者
NPR　p. 20 *l*. 6 参照

4 The fish moved autonomously for over 108 days, which is

25　equivalent to 38 million beats, the study states. Because heart cells constantly rebuild themselves, which takes about 20 days, Parker tells *NPR* the fish cells rebuilt themselves a total of about five times over.

5 Several years ago, Parker, who is interested in pediatric

30　heart disease, was frustrated by the state of heart therapeutics, he told *The Daily Beast's* Neel V. Patel.

pediatric　小児（科）の

6 "It occurred to me in 2007 that we might have failed to understand the fundamental laws of muscular pumps," he said in a 2012 statement. He began looking at marine

organisms for inspiration. Then, on a trip to the aquarium
with his daughter, he spotted a jellyfish.

7 "I'm looking at it, and thinking, 'It pumps, it looks like a
heart pump,' " he tells *The Daily Beast*. "I'm thinking, 'I
could build that damn thing.' "

8 In 2012, his team created a jellyfish that swam using rat
heart cells, and then a ray fish with rat heart cells in 2016.
The new biohybrid fish built off this previous research, per a
statement.

9 Though the researchers say the fish is a step forward for
heart research, it could be years before it leads to the
creation of an artificial heart, Michael Schneider, a professor
of regenerative cardiology at Imperial College London, who
was not involved in the study, tells *Insider*'s Marianne
Guenot. He tells the publication that the transplantation of
genetically altered pig hearts is more promising.

10 But that doesn't discourage Parker.

11 "I think that other methods will be faster than us,"
Parker tells *Insider*. "But in the long run, creating tissue that
relies on the patient's own cells could offer unexpected
benefits over pig organs or synthetic alternatives."

Notes

spot　目をとめる

damn thing　〈俗語〉こいつ

ray　エイ

biohybrid　生体（細胞）と機械部品を組み合わせて作られた
build off (=build on)
～に基づく

regenerative cardiology
再生心臓病学
Imperial College London
インペリアル・カレッジ・ロンドン
Insider　インサイダー、米オンライン経済メディア

Extra Notes

l. 21 bioengineering：生物工学。生物について広く学び、その研究成果を実社会（食料・医療・環境など）に応用する学問分野　*l.* 31 *The Daily Beast*：デイリー・ビースト、政治とポップカルチャーを主に扱う米ニュースサイト

Comprehension Questions

A 記事の内容に一致するものには T(True)、一致しないものには F(False)に丸をつけ、判断の基準になったパラグラフの番号を（　）に書き込みましょう。ただし、基準とするパラグラフは複数ある場合もあります。

1. The researcher's final goal is to build a heart for a sick kid.　　　**T / F** (　　　　)

2. Kit Parker, who is interested in pediatric heart disease, began looking at marine organisms for inspiration.　　　**T / F** (　　　　)

3. A professor who was not involved in the study says it could take years before an artificial heart is created.　　　**T / F** (　　　　)

4. An artificial fish that uses the contractions of human heart cells to swim autonomously has been engineered by scientists for the study of robotic fish.　　　**T / F** (　　　　)

5. The fish survived for more than three months and the fish cells rebuilt themselves five times or more.　　　**T / F** (　　　　)

B 以下は記事の要約です。適切な語を空所に書き入れ、音声を聞いて答えを確認しましょう。

DL 14　　CD 1-77

　　In order to improve the (**d**　　　　　¹) of artificial hearts for humans, scientists have engineered a (**s**　　　　　²) of fish that uses the contractions of human heart cells to swim autonomously. The fish, made with paper, gelatin, two layers of (**c**　　　　　³) muscle tissue and a plastic (**f**　　　　　⁴), is propelled through the water by muscle contractions. A contraction on one side caused the muscle on the other side to stretch, and the (**s**　　　　　⁵) then (**t**　　　　　⁶) those cells to contract, which moved the tail (**f**　　　　　⁷) side to side and allowed the fish to swim on its own. The fish moved autonomously for over 108 days, during which fish cells rebuilt themselves almost five times. Prior to this study, his team created a (**j**　　　　　⁸) that swam using rat heart cells, and then a (**r**　　　　　⁹) fish with rat heart cells. The (**s**　　　　　¹⁰) author of the paper, Kit Parker says "(**u**　　　　　¹¹), I want to build a heart for a sick kid."

Read Better, Understand More!

前置詞 2

　本Unitでも Readingの本文中、約60 ものワードが前置詞でした。中でもダントツに多いのがofで、13回登場しています。ざっくり言えばofは「の」という意味で、以下の例のように訳せます。

a school of fish	「一群の魚」
contractions of human heart cells	「ヒトの心臓細胞の収縮」
development of artificial hearts	「人工心臓の開発」
two layers of cardiac muscle tissue	「２層の心筋組織」

　しかし、英作文の際は日本語の「の」がofになるとは限りません。例えば、本文ではハーバード大学の教授はa professor at Harvard、インペリアル・カレッジ・ロンドンの教授はa professor at Imperial College Londonのように、場所を示す前置詞atを用いて表現されています。同様に「私はABC大学の学生です」という場合、日本ではofを使ってI am a student of ABC Universityと表現する人がほとんどですが、欧米ではI am a student at ABC Universityと表現する人が多いのです。

　Unit 8で取り上げなかったbyと withについて説明します。

　手段や方法を表すときに用いられるのがbyと withですが、byはそれを行った主体（人）あるいは手段（方法など）を示すときに、withはそれを行うのに用いた道具や物質を示すときに使います。

an autonomous pacing node acted like a pacemaker by controlling the rhythm
「自律性のペーシングノードはリズムをコントロールすることでペースメーカーのように働いた」

a ray fish with rat heart cells	「ネズミの心臓の細胞を使ったエイ」

Exercise

日本語と同じ意味になるように、空欄に適切な前置詞を入れなさい。

1. A氏は理学部化学科の教授である。

Mr. A is a professor (　　　　　　　) the Chemistry Department of the Faculty of Science.

2. トムは石でその窓ガラスを割った。

The window glass was broken (　　　　　　　) a stone (　　　　　　　) Tom.

3. ろ過するときは折りたたみろ紙を使いなさい。

Filtration should be carried out (　　　　　　　) folded filter paper.

After You Read

🎧 DL 15　💿 CD 1-78

A 会話を聞き、空所を埋めましょう。その後、会話をペアで練習しましょう。

Jacob: ¹_____. Harvard scientists produced an

artificial fish from human heart cells, and it swam in the water for more than three months!

Mia: Three months is really something. I wonder if those cells ²_____

_____.

Jacob: Looks like it. Otherwise, they cannot survive for such a long time.

Mia: How does it swim?

Jacob: The article says "the artificial fish ³_____

human heart cells to move the plastic tail from side to side and swim freely in water."

Mia: So it is a ⁴_____ and a

plastic part.

Jacob: The team had already created a jellyfish and a ray fish ⁵_____

_____, and this time they built a zebrafish-like biohybrid fish

from human heart cells.

Mia: But why heart cells?

Jacob: Since their ultimate goal is to produce artificial hearts for sick children.

B 以下の①と②の問題に答えましょう。

① 以下の例を見て、自分の言葉で文章の空所を埋めましょう。

ex) Ultimately, they want to produce artificial hearts for sick children.

「最終的に彼らは病気の子どもたちのために人工心臓を作りたいと思っている」

→ Their ultimate goal is to produce artificial hearts for sick children.

「彼らの究極の目標は、病気の子どもたちのために人工心臓を作ることだ」

My ultimate goal is ¹_____. To achieve my dream,

²_____.

② ①で書いた内容を元にクラスメートと話し合いましょう。

Behind the Scenes　バイオハイブリッド (biohybrid)

バイオハイブリッドは、「生体細胞と無機物を融合させた」という意味です。本文には、ヒトの幹細胞を分化させて作った心筋細胞、プラスチック、ゼラチンを材料とし、ゼブラフィッシュの形に作り上げた魚が登場しました。この人工魚は水中に溶けた糖などの栄養分を表面から吸収して成長し、108日間にわたり水中を泳ぎました。時間とともに泳ぐ速度も向上し、最終的に自然に生息するゼブラフィッシュ並みの速度に達したのです。

誰かがスマホをチェックし始めると、無意識のうちにあなたも電話を取り出しているかもしれません。あくびが伝染するように、スマホチェックも伝染することが最近の研究でわかりました。これはカメレオン効果と呼ばれる現象で、カメレオンが環境に合わせて体色を変化させるように、私たちも周囲で生じていることに合わせて行動を変えているのです。

Research Shows Checking Your Phone Is Contagious Like Yawning

Before You Read

A 日本語の意味に合うように、空所に適切な語を語群から選んで書きましょう。語群には１つ余分なものがあります。

1. 同じ心理現象が人々に影響をおよぼしている

the same psychological (　　　　　　　　　　　) influences people

2. スマホを見ることはせずに、ただそれを手でいじった

just (　　　　　　　　　) with a smartphone without looking at it

3. 私たちは課せられた規範にしたがう必要がある

we have a need to follow the norms (　　　　　　　　　) on us

4. スマホは社会的孤立を増加させる可能性がある

smartphones can increase social (　　　　　　　　)

5. 全員が等しくカメレオン効果のもつ影響を受けやすかった。

everyone was equally (　　　　　　　　　　) to the chameleon effect's impulse

> phenomenon susceptible fiddled imposed isolation primary

B 下線部の英語の意味として適切な日本語を空所に書きましょう。

1. researchers <u>interacted with</u> their smartphone　研究者は自分のスマホと (　　　　　　　)

2. disruption with <u>ongoing</u> activities　　(　　　　　　　　　) 活動の中断

3. people often <u>pick up</u> each other's mood　人はしばしば互いの気分に (　　　　　　)

4. yawns are so <u>contagious</u>　　　　あくびはとても (　　　　　　)

5. <u>odds</u> that people will use their phones　人々が電話を使用するであろう (　　　　　　)

Reading

🅞 CD 1-79 〜 🅞 CD 1-89

Notes

|1| A study published last month in *the Journal of Ethology*
suggests the same psychological phenomenon that makes
yawns contagious also influences people to check their
smartphones, reports *The Guardian*.

5 |2| During the experiment, a researcher either looked at and
interacted with their smartphone, or just fiddled with the
phone without looking at it. Then they looked around for 30
seconds, counting up the number of people around who
started using their phones, too.

10 |3| The study shows that after the first person starts to use
their phone, about half of the people around them check their
phones, too.

|4| "We have a need to follow the norms imposed on us by
people around us, to [match] our actions with theirs in this

15 automatic way," says Elisabetta Palagi, a social behavior
expert at the University of Pisa, to Christa Lesté-Lasserre at
New Scientist. "But smartphones can increase social isolation
through interference and disruption with real-life, ongoing
activities."

20 |5| The study looked at phone use as an example of the
chameleon effect, which is the way people change their
behavior to match what's happening around them. This is
why people often pick up each others' mood or gestures
during a conversation, and why yawns are so contagious.

25 |6| The researchers usually took on the role of the "trigger,"
or the person who checked their phone first. They tested the
two versions of phone-use—looking or not looking—in a
variety of settings, like in waiting rooms, at work, at
restaurants or at home. The trigger person recorded the

30 effect glancing at their phone had on their neighbors, as well
as characteristics like the others' ages and relationship to
the trigger person.

|7| Out of about 100 people who saw both versions of phone
use, everyone was equally susceptible to the chameleon

the Journal of Ethology
学術出版のシュプリンガー社が
発行している動物行動学の
ジャーナル

social behavior
社会的行動

New Scientist
p.8 *l*.13参照
real-life
現実世界の

look at
検討する、考察する

35 effect's impulse to check their phone.

8 "Most people get infected by other people's mobile phone behavior, without even realizing it," says Palagi to *New Scientist*.

9 The odds that people nearby would use their phones were
40 about 28 times higher when the first user actually looked at their phone while they used it, compared to when the trigger person just held the phone and tapped it without looking. That suggests that the goal of interacting with whatever's onscreen is what inspires people to pick up their own phones,
45 and not just the movement of picking up a phone and tapping the screen.

10 For now, the effect seems both quick and subconscious, at least anecdotally.

11 "One woman who was sitting across from me in a waiting
50 room saw me check my phone," says University of Pisa biologist Veronica Maglieri, a co-author on the study, to *New Scientist*. "Within seconds she took out her phone and called someone and said, 'Hey, I just felt like calling you; I don't know why.'"

Comprehension Questions

A 記事の内容に一致するものには T (True)、一致しないものには F (False) に丸をつけ、判断の基準になったパラグラフの番号を（ ）に書き込みましょう。ただし、基準とするパラグラフは複数ある場合もあります。

1. The chameleon effect can explain why yawns are so contagious. **T / F** (   )

2. When the first user actually looked at their phone while they used it, probably less people would use their phones, compared to when the trigger person just held the phone and tapped it without looking. **T / F** (   )

3. An expert says smartphones can make people socially isolated. **T / F** (   )

4. The reason why most people get infected by other's mobile phone behavior is that behavior reminds them of their phone. **T / F** (   )

5. In this research the trigger means the person who checked their phone first. **T / F** (   )

B 以下は記事の要約です。適切な語を空所に書き入れ、音声を聞いて答えを確認しましょう。

🎧 DL 16   💿 CD 1-90

A study published last month suggests the same (**p**   [1]) phenomenon that (**m**   [2]) yawns contagious also influences people to check their smart-phones. When a person starts to use their phone, about half of the people around them will start (**c**   [3]) their phones within 30 seconds. The study looked at phone use as an example of the chameleon effect, which is the way people change their (**b**   [4]) to match what's happening around them. This is why people often (**p**   [5]) up each others' mood or (**g**   [6]) during a conversation, and why yawns are so contagious. For now, the effect seems both quick and (**s**   [7]).

Read Better, Understand More!

数量表現 1

　科学英語では定性的な表現より定量的な表現が好まれます。AとBの重さを比べ、その差が3kgだったとき、これを定性的に表すと「AはBよりかなり重い（A is quite heavier than B）」となりますが、定量的に表現すると「AはBより3kg重い（A is 3 kg heavier than B）」となります。

　さて、本文には以下のような一文がありました。

The odds that people nearby would use their phones were about 28 times higher when the first user actually looked at their phone while they used it, compared to when the trigger person just held the phone and tapped it without looking.
「トリガー役の人がただ電話を持って、それを見ずに軽く叩いているときに比べ、最初の使用者（＝トリガー役の人）が電話を使う間、実際にそれを見ていたときには、近くの人が電話を使用するであろう確率は約28倍に高まった」

　ここでは

when the first user actually looked at their phone while they used it
「最初の使用者が電話を使う間、実際にそれを見ていたとき」

when the trigger person just held the phone and tapped it without looking
「トリガー役の人がただ電話を持っているだけで、それを見ずに軽く叩いているとき」

　という2つの状況を比較し、前者の方がpeople nearby would use their phonesの確率が約28倍高かったと言っているのですが、比較する部分が長いのでthanではなくcompared to が用いられています。

Exercise

次の文に（　　　）内の数字を入れて、より科学的な表現にしましょう。

1. He is much older than I. （50歳）

_____

2. I get up much earlier than my sister. （2時間）

_____

3. I used to weigh much less than I do now. （10 kg）

_____

After You Read

A 会話を聞き、空所を埋めましょう。その後、会話をペアで練習しましょう。

Brian: Have you ever heard of the chameleon effect?

Mary: It is **1**_____ to match
what's happening around them, isn't it? I learned it in my psychology class.

Brian: According to a new study, checking smartphones is an example of the chameleon effect.
2_____.

Mary: You mean, seeing people checking their phones **3**_____
_____ our phones, too?

Brian: Nope. We do so unconsciously. Imagine a lady sitting across from you starts checking
her phone. Then, without even noticing, **4**_____
_____ and say "Hey, I just felt like calling you, I don't know why."

Mary: Gee, **5**_____! What
is the name of this academic discipline?

Brian: It is called ethology*.

*ethology：動物行動学

B 以下の①と②の問題に答えましょう。

①　以下の例を見て、自分の言葉で文章の空所を埋めましょう。

ex) I saw people (①check/②checking/③checked) their phones.
私は人々がスマホを（①チェックする／②チェックしている／③チェックした）のを見た。

私が見た時に
- ①＝人々がスマホをチェックしているか、チェックし終えた場合
- ②＝人々がスマホをチェックしている最中の場合
- ③＝人々はスマホをチェックし終わっている場合

I hear a bird **1**_____.
I saw the gate **2**_____.

②　①で書いた内容を元にクラスメートと話し合いましょう。

Behind the Scenes　カメレオン効果

カメレオン効果とは、別名ミラーリングとも呼ばれ、無意識に他人の行動などを真似てしまう現象のことです。よく知られているのは、1人があくびをすると、その周りの人が次々にあくびをする、あくびの伝染です。ところで、意図的にミラーリングを行い、相手の仕草や行動を真似すると、真似された相手はこちらに好感を持つことが実験でわかっています。誰かと信頼関係を築きたいときには、これを利用することもできそうです。

死体花とも呼ばれるショクダイオオコンニャクは、10年に1度しか花を咲かせない変わった植物ですが、今その数は少なく絶滅の危機に瀕しています。現在世界中に約1,500株が残っていますが、近くに生息するものは互いに近親関係にあり、同系交配による種子は育ちにくいからです。そこで植物園は血統台帳を作り、遠方の植物園と協力し、死体花の人工授粉に乗り出しました。

UNIT 9

To Save the Corpse Flower, Horticulturists Are Playing the Role of Matchmakers

Before You Read

A 日本語の意味に合うように、空所に適切な語を語群から選んで書きましょう。語群には1つ余分なものがあります。

1. 野生でも植物園においても、死体花の生存を脅かす
threaten the corpse flower's existence in both the wild and in (　　　　　　　) gardens

2. 同系交配の植物は生存能力のない種子を作り出す
inbred plants produce (　　　　　　　) seeds

3. 難貯蔵性種子は生き残るために水を必要とする
recalcitrant seeds need water to (　　　　　　　)

4. 動物は難貯蔵性種子を食べ、その後糞として排出する
animals eat recalcitrant seeds and then (　　　　　　　) them in their scat

5. 死体花は無性生殖と有性生殖の両方が可能である
corpse flowers can (　　　　　　　) both asexually and sexually

> expel botanic feces reproduce survive unviable

B 下線部の英語の意味として適切な日本語を空所に書きましょう。

1. captivating the world since its discovery　　発見されて以来、世界を（　　　　　　　）
2. when conditions are optimal　　条件が（　　　　　　　）ときに
3. flowers are all too closely related　　花はすべてあまりにも近い（　　　　　　　）
4. spearhead a project　　プロジェクトの（　　　　　　　）
5. plants native to hot and humid climates　　高温多湿な地域が（　　　　　　　）植物

Notes

Amorphophallus titanium
ショクダイオオコンニャク

botanist　植物学者

1　The corpse flower, *Amorphophallus titanium*, has been captivating the world since its discovery in 1878 by Italian botanist Odoardo Beccari. This rare and unusual plant only blooms about once every decade (or longer) when conditions

5　are optimal, leading to a shallow genetic pool threatening the corpse flower's existence in both the wild and in botanic gardens, reports Doug Johnson for *Undark*.

2　With fewer than 1,000 individuals left in the wild and 500 specimens living in private and public botanic

10　collections, genetic diversity is limited, and these flowers are all too closely related. Inbred plants produce unviable seeds, which could potentially eliminate any hope of preservation, reports Samantha Drake for *The New York Times*.

3　In 2019, the Chicago Botanic Garden spearheaded a

15　project called "Tools and Resources for Endangered and Exceptional Plant Species," or TREES for short, to create a studbook-like database that other botanic gardens can use to preserve endangered plant species, reports *Undark*. Jeremie Frant, a conservation scientist at the Chicago Botanic

20　Garden, tells *The New York Times* that project developers chose a total of six rare plant species to preserve, including the corpse flower, that produce seeds that can't survive traditional seed storing methods or don't produce enough seeds naturally.

25　4　Most of the plants in the TREES project have recalcitrant seeds, meaning they can't withstand freezing or drying methods used in seed banks and die. Recalcitrant seeds need water to survive, and in the wild, animals eat recalcitrant seeds and then expel them in their scat. Tropical

30　plants native to hot and humid climates tend to have recalcitrant seeds.

5　Corpse flowers can reproduce both asexually and sexually. When they reproduce asexually, they produce multiple plants that get sent out to botanic gardens, but they

specimen　見本、実例
genetic diversity
遺伝的多様性

studbook
（動物〈特に馬〉の）血統台帳

conservation　保全

recalcitrant seeds
難貯蔵性種子。乾燥、冷凍によって発芽能力を失う種子。

56

lack genetic diversity through this method of reproduction, reports *Undark*. A corpse flower only blooms for 24 to 36 hours before the blossom collapses. During this time, botanists need to pollinate it artificially to produce more offspring and genetic variation. Scientists also use this time to collect pollen to share with other botanical gardens. The Chicago Botanic Garden has also started to save pollen to send to other gardens worldwide for cross-pollination for a national corpse flower conservation project.

6 In July 2020, a corpse flower named "Sprout" at the Longwood Botanical Gardens in Kennett Square, Pennsylvania bloomed for the second time after it first bloomed in 2016 at the Chicago Botanic Garden, Elaine Ayers reported for *Atlas Obscura* this past summer. Sprout arrived at the Longwood Botanical Gardens in 2018, and from there, Longwood's senior horticulturist Joyce Rondinella cared for Sprout. Pollen was collected when Sprout bloomed, and soon after, the plant was artificially pollinated by a human, a role beetles would normally play in the wild.

7 "We at botanic gardens have to work together to save some species," Frant tells *Undark*. "Because we can't do it on our own."

Notes

pollinate 授粉する

offspring 子、子孫

pollen 花粉

cross-pollination
異花（他花）授粉

sprout 芽

horticulturist 園芸家

on one's own
p.14 *l*. 11 参照

Extra Notes

l. 7 *Undark*：「真実、美、科学」をキャッチフレーズとする非営利のデジタルマガジン *l.* 48 *Atlas Obscura*：米国ベースのオンラインマガジン（ウェブサイトに掲載される記事は科学、歴史、食べ物など様々なトピックをカバーしている）

Comprehension Questions

A 記事の内容に一致するものには T(True)、一致しないものには F(False)に丸をつけ、判断の基準になったパラグラフの番号を（　）に書き込みましょう。ただし、基準とするパラグラフは複数ある場合もあります。

1. When plants too closely related to each other mate, they produce more viable seeds.

   T / F （　　　　）

2. Recalcitrant seeds are difficult to preserve during storage since they can't withstand freezing or drying methods used in seed banks and die.　　　 T / F （　　　　）

3. Just like other flowering plants, corpse flowers reproduce sexually through a process called pollination, and it is the only way for them to survive.　　　 T / F （　　　　）

4. In 2020, when a corpse flower named "Sprout" bloomed for the second time after it first bloomed in 2016, pollen was collected and soon after, the plant was artificially pollinated by a human.　　　 T / F （　　　　）

5. The TREES project creates a database which can be used by other botanic gardens to preserve endangered plant species.　　　 T / F （　　　　）

B 以下は記事の要約です。適切な語を空所に書き入れ、音声を聞いて答えを確認しましょう。

🎧 DL 18　　⦿ CD 2-08

　　The corpse flower only (**b**　　　　　　¹) about once every decade when conditions are (**o**　　　　　　²). With fewer than 1,500 (**i**　　　　　　³) living in the world, (**g**　　　　　　⁴) diversity is limited, (**t**　　　　　　⁵) the corpse flower's (**e**　　　　　　⁶). Besides, these flowers are all too closely related and the (**i**　　　　　　⁷) plants produce (**u**　　　　　　⁸) seeds. The seeds of the corpse flower are called recalcitrant seeds, which are difficult to preserve during storage, as they need water to survive. (**T**　　　　　　⁹) plants native to hot and humid (**c**　　　　　　¹⁰) tend to have recalcitrant seeds. In 2019, the Chicago Botanic Garden (**s**　　　　　　¹¹) a project called "Tools and Resources for Endangered and Exceptional Plant Species," or TREES for short, to create a database that other botanic gardens can use to preserve endangered plant species. People at botanic gardens will work together to save these species since they can't do it on their (**o**　　　　　　¹²).

Read Better, Understand More!

数量表現 2

　科学の世界で厳密に表現するとき、more thanは「〜以上」、less thanは「〜以下」ではありません。次の例を見てください。

more than 10 kg 　　　　　　　「10kgより重い（10 kgは含まず）」
less than 5 kg 　　　　　　　　「5 kg未満」

　年齢を表す場合は、lessやyoungerの代わりにunder the age ofを使用することもできます。

less than 6 years old = younger than 6 years old = under the age of 6

　本文に登場した数量表現を見てみましょう。

fewer than 1,000 individuals 　「個体（数）が1,000未満」
once every decade (or longer) 　「10年に1回（＝10年毎に）（またはそれ以上の間隔で）」

　or longerは「〜以上」に相当する表現になります。つまり10 kg以上は10 kg or moreとなるのです。ただし、日常生活における表現では、それほど厳密ではなく「〜以上」の意味でmore thanを使っている場合もあります。

Exercise

日本語の意味に合う様に、空所に適切な語を書きましょう。

1. 23 kgを超える重量超過手荷物
   overweight baggage weighing (　　　　　　) (　　　　　　　　) 23 kg
2. 3年に一度のお祭り
   a festival held (　　　　　　) (　　　　　　) (　　　　　　)
3. 18歳未満の少年少女
   minors (　　　　　　) (　　　　　　) (　　　　　　) (　　　　　　) 18

After You Read

DL 19 · CD 2-09

A 会話を聞き、空所を埋めましょう。その後、会話をペアで練習しましょう。

Alex: I went to Tsukuba Botanical Garden to see the corpse flower bloom. This flower normally blooms about once every decade, but there it bloomed after **1** _____ _____ ! The flower smelled like rotting flesh, hence **2** _____ .

Grace: Wow. As I recall, the corpse flower is one of the plant species in the TREES project.

Alex: What does TREES stand for?

Grace: Tools and Resources for Endangered and Exceptional Plant Species. Horticulturists are now creating a studbook-like database that other **3** _____ _____ endangered plant species.

Alex: I see. The studbook-like database will provide information on the ancestor of each flower, right? That will be **4** _____ . In fact, how many individuals still exist globally?

Grace: Only 500 specimens are living in botanic collections, but I heard the Chicago Botanic Garden **5** _____ to other gardens for cross-pollination.

B 以下の①と②の問題に答えましょう。

① 以下の例を見て、自分の言葉で文章の空所を埋めましょう。

    ex) *Your friend:* What does TREES stand for?「TREESって何の略」

        You: It stands for Tools and Resources for Endangered and Exceptional Plant Species.「Tools and Resources for Endangered and Exceptional Plant Speciesの略だよ」

        Your friend: What does **1** (MBA / ABC / JR / NASA / NEET / TOEIC / WHO / JPN / MRI /, etc. [自分で思い浮かんだ略語]) stand for?

        You: It means **2** _____ .

② ①で書いた略語をテーマにクラスメートと話し合いましょう。

Behind the Scenes   死体花（ショクダイオオコンニャク）とは

スマトラ島原産の世界最大級の花。開花すると強烈な腐敗臭を出し、2日間の開花中、動物の死体を餌とする甲虫（シデムシ）を引き寄せます。仏炎苞（クルリと巻いた花弁のように見えるもの）に着地した虫は、這い上がれずに転がり落ち、雌花の柱頭に体に付着した他の花の花粉をなすりつけ、翌日雌花の受粉機能が停止すると、雄花から花粉が溢れ出して虫に降り注ぎます。花は枯れ、中に閉じ込められていた甲虫は花粉を体につけ脱出し、別の花へと向かうのです。受粉した雌花は果実をつけ、鳥がそれを食べて種子を撒きます。

UNIT 10

走る、飛ぶ、跳ぶ。これまでロボットの動きは人や動物の体の仕組みを参考に開発されてきましたが、生物には筋肉のもつ限界があります。発想を変えて作られたこの一本足のジャンパーは、過去のロボットがもつ記録をはるかに上回り、30mの跳躍が可能です。重力の小さい月の上では1回のジャンプで、500メートルを移動することも可能になるでしょう。

Robot Jumps a Record-Breaking 100 Feet in the Air

▌Before You Read

Ⓐ 日本語の意味に合うように、空所に適切な語を語群から選んで書きましょう。語群には1つ余分なものがあります。

1. この技術は地球上や宇宙で障害物を回避して進むのに使用することができる

this technology could be used to (   ) obstacles on earth and in space

2. この装置は現在の記録の3倍以上も跳びあがることができる

the device can (   ) three times higher than the current record

3. 多くの機械系の跳躍システムは生物学的な跳躍体に基づいている

many (   ) jumping systems are based on biological jumpers

4. 筋肉による1打（撃）でどれだけのエネルギーを作り出せるかに基づいた

based on how much energy they can produce in a (   ) of their muscle

5. 停止状態からおよそ2.3メートルの高さまで跳び上がるのが測定されている

which has been measured jumping around 2.3 meters high from a (   )

> stroke　leap　standstill　navigate　mechanical　triple

Ⓑ 下線部の英語の意味として適切な日本語を空所に書きましょう。

1. have <u>limits</u> to their jumping ability　　　かれらの跳躍能力には（　　　　　）がある

2. a release mechanism <u>is unlatched</u>　　　リリース機構を（　　　　　）

3. this device's <u>spring-to-motor</u> ratio　　　この装置の（　　　　　）比

4. larger than B <u>by about 100 times</u>　　　Bの（　　　　　）大きい

5. <u>cover</u> half a kilometer in a single bound　　　一回のジャンプで0.5km（　　　　　）

Reading

CD 2-10 ～ CD 2-18

Notes

[1] Researchers at the University of California, Santa Barbara have designed a one-foot device that can leap more than 100 feet in the air—three times the current record for a jumping robot, according to a video. The paper, which was
5 published in the journal *Nature*, suggests this technology could be used to navigate obstacles on earth and in space.

University of California, Santa Barbara　カリフォルニア大学サンタバーバラ校
one-foot　1本足の

[2] "The motivation came from a scientific question," lead author Elliot W. Hawkes, a mechanical engineer at UC Santa Barbara, says in a statement. "We wanted to understand
10 what the limits were on engineered jumpers."

lead author　筆頭著者

[3] Many mechanical jumping systems are based on biological jumpers—or those in the animal kingdom. But animals have limits to their jumping ability based on how much energy they can produce in a stroke of their muscle,
15 Charles Xaio, a researcher in Hawkes' lab, says in the statement. Animals have relatively small springs too — just enough to store the energy produced by this stroke.

[4] "The best animal jumper is likely [a squirrel-sized primate called] the galago, which has been measured
20 jumping around 2.3 meters [10.5 feet] high from a standstill," Hawkes tells *Scientific American*'s Sophie Bushwick.

primate　霊長類

Scientific American
p.8 *l*. 21 参照

[5] Researchers in this study took a different approach, using a motor to take multiple strokes and increase the amount of stored energy in the spring. The small motor
25 winds up a line that constricts the spring, which is made of carbon-fiber compression bows and rubber bands. When a release mechanism is unlatched, the device launches into the air.

constrict　収縮させる
compression　圧縮

[6] Because the stored energy is greater, this device's spring-
30 to-motor ratio was also larger than what's seen in the animal kingdom by about 100 times, per the statement. The device is lightweight and aerodynamic, which allows it to jump the height of a 10-story building and accelerate from zero to 60 mph in 9 ms.

aerodynamic
空気力学の（原理を応用した）
accelerate
加速する、速度が加わる
mph [mile per hour (m/h)]
時速（1時間当たり）～マイル
ms　ミリ秒、1000分の1秒

35 **7** "It jumps much higher than most of the rest of the jumping robots in the world do—if not all of them that I'm aware of," Sarah Bergbreiter, a mechanical engineer at Carnegie Mellon University, who was not involved in the new study but wrote a commentary about it, tells *Scientific*
40 *American*.

8 While this kind of device could be used to navigate difficult terrains on earth, researchers say it could reach heights even greater on the moon, where gravity is weaker.

9 "On Earth, jumping robots could overcome obstacles
45 previously only navigated by flying robots while collecting vision-based data of the ground below," write the authors. "On the Moon, the leaps of the presented jumper would be even loftier: 125 m [410 ft] high while covering half a kilometer [0.3 miles] in a single bound."

Notes

Carnegie Mellon University
カーネギーメロン大学

terrain 地形、地勢

lofty 非常に高い

Extra Notes

l. 2 leap：跳ぶ（jumpは跳躍の動作に、leapは跳躍による移動に重点がおかれる）
l. 5 *Nature*：ネイチャー誌。イギリスを拠点とする国際的な週刊総合学術雑誌

Comprehension Questions

A 記事の内容に一致するものには T（True）、一致しないものには F（False）に丸をつけ、判断の基準になったパラグラフの番号を（　）に書き込みましょう。ただし、基準とするパラグラフは複数ある場合もあります。

1. Biological jumpers have been models for mechanical jumping systems, but animals have limits to their jumping ability based on the amount of energy they can produce in a stroke of their muscle. **T / F** (　　　　)

2. Sarah Bergbreiter, a mechanical engineer at Carnegie Mellon University, says the device jumps much higher than any of the jumping robots in the world. **T / F** (　　　　)

3. The best animal jumper is likely a kind of small squirrel and it can jump 2.3 meters high from a standstill. **T / F** (　　　　)

4. On the Moon, the leaps of the device would be 4 times the height it reaches on Earth. **T / F** (　　　　)

5. The research started when researchers wanted to understand what the limits were on biological jumpers. **T / F** (　　　　)

B 以下は記事の要約です。適切な語を空所に書き入れ、音声を聞いて答えを確認しましょう。

DL 20　CD 2-19

Researchers at the University of California, Santa Barbara have designed a (o　　　　　　¹) device that can (l　　　　　　²) more than 100 feet in the air—three times the (c　　　　　　³) record for a jumping robot. Many mechanical jumping systems are based on biological jumpers. But animals have limits to their jumping ability based on how much energy they can produce in a stroke of their muscle. Animals have (r　　　　　　⁴) small (s　　　　　　⁵) too — just enough to store the energy produced by this stroke. Researchers used a (m　　　　　　⁶) to take (m　　　　　　⁷) strokes and (i　　　　　　⁸) the amount of stored energy in the spring. The device is lightweight and (a　　　　　　⁹), which allows it to jump the height of a 10-story building and accelerate from zero to 60 mph in 9 ms. This technology could be used to (n　　　　　　¹⁰) obstacles on earth and in space.

Read Better, Understand More!

数量表現 3

本文に登場した数量に関する表現を見てみたいと思います。まずは1つ目です。

three times higher than the current record 「現在の記録の3倍高く」

「～倍」はtimesを使って表現することができます。形容詞の部分は比較級を使っても良いですし、原級を使った表現（as～as）も可能です。また「2倍」は以下の例のようにtwiceを使って表現できます。

I ate twice as much cake as he did. 「私はケーキを彼の2倍食べた」

単位を使う際は『動詞＋数字＋単位＋形容詞』の形で表現できます。（ここで1つ注意。単位は、数字が1以外のときは1より大きくても、1より小さくても必ず複数形で表します。）

jump 2.3 meters high 「2.3メートルの高さに跳び上がる」

こちらと同じ内容を、使われている形容詞の名詞形を使って、以下のように表現することもできます。

jump to a height of 2.3 meters

こちらでは『動詞＋（前置詞＋）a＋名詞形＋of＋数字＋単位』の形で表現されています。名詞形の例として、他にwidth, lengthなどがあります。前置詞を使わない例としては次のものがあります。

leap a height of 100 feet 「100フィートの高さに跳び上がる」

量の増減の程度を表すときには前置詞 by を使います。

larger than what's seen in the animal kingdom by about 100 times
「動物の世界で見られるものの約100倍大きい」

差を表すときにも使えるので、以下の英文のような表現が可能です。

My annual income increased by 1 million yen from last year.
「私の年収は去年より100万円増えた」

Exercise

日本語と同じ意味になるように、英文を完成させましょう。

1. このしおりの厚みは1.5ミリだ。

This bookmark has (　　　　　　　　) (　　　　　　　　　　　)
(　　　　　　　　) (　　　　　　　　) (　　　　　　　　　).

2. 私は彼の5倍働く。

I work (　　　　　　　) (　　　　　　　) (　　　　　　　)
(　　　　　　) (　　　　　　　) he does.

3. 接着強度はアルカリを添加すると3倍に増加した。

The adhesive strength was increased (　　　　　　　　)
(　　　　　　) (　　　　　　　　) when an alkali was added.

After You Read

DL 21   CD 2-20

A 会話を聞き、空所を埋めましょう。その後、会話をペアで練習しましょう。

Ryan: Look, here is an interesting article. The ¹_____

_____ was broken! The robot created by the researchers at the University of

California can leap more than 30 meters in the air.

Ellie: Wow, if the robot can leap more than 30 meters, it must be very light. ²_____

_____?

Ryan: Certainly it is small and light. The length is 30 centimeters and ³_____

_____. This robot is a one-foot jumper with a small motor, carbon-fiber

compression bows and rubber bands.

Ellie: And what on earth will it be used for?

Ryan: It can navigate difficult terrains on earth and collect vision-based data of the ground

below. Or it will be more useful on the Moon, where the gravity ⁴_____

_____ the Earth; it can leap 125 meters high and cover 500 meters. Since

airplanes cannot fly without air, jumping ⁵_____

_____ on the Moon where there's no air.

B 以下の1と2の問題に答えましょう。

1 以下の例を見て、自分の言葉で文章の空所を埋めましょう。

　　ex) What on earth will it be used for?「それは一体何に使われるの」

　　　→ What in the name of wonder will it be used for?「それは一体何に使われるの」

　　　→ What in the world will it be used for?「それは一体何に使われるの」

　　What on earth ¹_____?

　　What in the name of wonder ²_____?

　　What in the world ³_____?

2 1で書いた文を使ってクラスメートと会話しましょう。

Behind the Scenes　　障害物を回避して進む

移動手段として車は大変便利ですが、表面に大きな凸凹がある険しい山や谷が続く地形を
通るのは困難です。また、飛行機やヘリコプターは、流体である空気の存在を必要とする
ので、宇宙空間では利用できません。その点、跳躍を利用した移動方法は、空気がない場
所であっても、深いクレーターなどの障害物を避けて移動ができます。また、月面などの
重力の小さい環境では、より高く、より長距離を跳ぶことができる利点があるのです。

UNIT 11

宇宙貧血と呼ばれる現象があります。宇宙空間で無重力におかれると、人体の赤血球の破壊が加速されるのです。体液シフトが関係しているとされるものの、詳細はまだ不明です。貧血の原因を厳密に突き止めることができれば、地上の患者にとっても治療や予防に役立つでしょう。まず科学者が提案しているのは宇宙食の改良です。

Space Is Destroying Astronauts' Red Blood Cells

Before You Read

A 日本語の意味に合うように、空所に適切な語を語群から選んで書きましょう。語群には 1 つ余分なものがあります。

1. 体は地上にいるときよりも速い速度で自らの血球を破壊している

bodies are destroying their own blood cells at higher (　　　　　　　　) than on Earth

2. これは全宇宙飛行期間中続く

this continues for the entire (　　　　　　　　) of the astronauts' mission

3. 宇宙飛行士はそのミッション中に 4 回のサンプルを採取した

astronauts took samples four times (　　　　　　　　) their missions

4. ヘム分子が一個破壊されるたびに一酸化炭素分子が一個生じる

a (　　　　　　　　) of CO is produced every time a (　　　　　　　　)
of heme is destroyed　※ この（　）には同じ単語が入ります。

5. 持久力、体力に影響を及ぼす貧血はミッションの目的を脅かす可能性がある

anemia affecting your (　　　　　　　　) and strength can threaten mission objectives

> during　duration　molecule　extract　endurance　rates

B 下線部の英語の意味として適切な日本語を空所に書きましょう。

1. space anemia has <u>consistently</u> been reported　宇宙貧血は（　　　　　　）報告されてきた

2. astronauts' bodies <u>undergo</u> fluid shifts　宇宙飛行士の体は体液シフトを（　　　　　　）

3. <u>thankfully</u>, it isn't a problem　（　　　　　　）それは問題ではない

4. when your body is <u>weightless</u>　あなたの体が（　　　　　　）とき

5. <u>followup</u> samples showed that ~　（　　　　　　）のサンプルは～を示した

Reading

	Notes
	take a toll on one's body 体に負担をかける

1 Space travel takes many tolls on the human body, and new research suggests long-duration flights are changing astronauts' blood. According to the study published in the journal *Nature Medicine*, astronauts' bodies are destroying
5 their own blood cells while in space at higher rates than on Earth.

Nature Medicine
Nature Publishing Groupが発行する医学に関する研究を掲載している学術誌

2 "Space anemia has consistently been reported when astronauts returned to Earth since the first space missions, but we didn't know why," says study author Guy Trudel, a
10 rehabilitation physician and researcher at The Ottawa Hospital and professor at the University of Ottawa in Canada, in a statement. "Our study shows that upon arriving in space, more red blood cells are destroyed, and this continues for the entire duration of the astronauts' mission."

physician 医師

15 3 In the study, researchers took breath and blood samples from 14 astronauts before their six-month stays on the International Space Station and collected blood from the astronauts up to a year after their spaceflight. The astronauts also took samples four times during their
20 missions. The team measured the amounts of carbon monoxide within the breath samples because a molecule of carbon monoxide is produced every time a molecule of heme, a component of red blood cells, is destroyed, explains Nick Lavars for *New Atlas*.

carbon monoxide
一酸化炭素

New Atlas 科学、技術、デザイン分野の情報を発信するオンラインマガジン

25 4 The results revealed that astronauts lost around 54 percent more red blood cells in space. While on Earth, our bodies create and destroy around 2 million red blood cells per second. But in space, astronauts lost 3 million red blood cells per second during their six-month missions. The scientists
30 say the reason red blood cells are being destroyed is likely due to fluid shifts the astronauts' bodies undergo to adjust to their weightless environment and back again.

5 "Thankfully, having fewer red blood cells in space isn't a problem when your body is weightless," says Trudel. "But

when landing on Earth and potentially on other planets or
moons, anemia affecting your energy, endurance and
strength can threaten mission objectives. The effects of
anemia are only felt once you land, and must deal with
gravity again."

[6] Even when the astronauts returned to Earth, their "space
anemia," didn't go away. Follow-up samples showed that their
red blood cell counts slowly returned to normal within three
to four months of their return. But samples collected a year
later revealed that the rate of red blood cell destruction was
still revved up—now around 30 percent above pre-spaceflight
levels, according to Ashley Strickland for *CNN*.

[7] To reduce the risk of anemia in space, the researchers
suggest tweaking astronaut diets to better support their
health needs. The finding is also important for non-
astronauts, as commercial spaceflight becomes more popular.

[8] "If we can find out exactly what's causing this anemia,
then there is a potential to treat it or prevent it, both for
astronauts and for patients here on Earth," says Trudel.

rev （速度）をあげる

tweak 微調整する

Extra Notes

l. 22 heme：赤血球の中に含まれ、酸素を運搬する働きをもつヘモグロビンの中心に存在する、鉄イオンを含む錯体（金属イオンに配位子と呼ばれる分子やイオンが結合したもの）

Comprehension Questions

A 記事の内容に一致するものには T(True)、一致しないものには F(False)に丸をつけ、判断の基準になったパラグラフの番号を（　）に書き込みましょう。ただし、基準とするパラグラフは複数ある場合もあります。

1. The team measured the amounts of carbon monoxide within the breath samples to find out how much heme, a component of red blood cells, was destroyed.   **T / F** (　　　)

2. People feel the effects of space anemia only once they are back on Earth and deal with gravity again.   **T / F** (　　　)

3. The number of astronauts' red blood cells returned to normal after they were back home, but the destruction rate was still high compared to the rate before they went to space.

   T / F (　　　)

4. Space anemia has never been reported when astronauts returned to Earth, and this is the first time for scientists to investigate it.   **T / F** (　　　)

5. The scientists have no idea about the reason astronauts' red blood cells are being destroyed in space.   **T / F** (　　　)

B 以下は記事の要約です。適切な語を空所に書き入れ、音声を聞いて答えを確認しましょう。

🎧 DL 22　⏺ CD 2-29

  Astronauts' bodies are destroying their (**o**　　　　　　　¹) blood cells while in space at higher (**r**　　　　　　　²) than on Earth. While on Earth, our bodies (**c**　　　　　　　³) and destroy around 2 million red blood cells per second, but in space, astronauts lose 3 million red blood cells per second. The scientists say the reason red blood cells are being destroyed may be (**d**　　　　　　　⁴) to fluid (**s**　　　　　　　⁵) the astronauts' bodies (**u**　　　　　　　⁶) in space. Space anemia isn't a problem when you are in space; its effects are only felt once you are back home and deal with gravity again. After coming back home, their red blood cell (**c**　　　　　　　⁷) slowly returned to normal but the rate of red blood cell destruction was still higher than the pre-(**s**　　　　　　　⁸) levels. To reduce the (**r**　　　　　　　⁹) of space anemia, the researchers suggest changing astronaut (**d**　　　　　　　¹⁰) to better support their health (**n**　　　　　　　¹¹).

Read Better, Understand More!

複合名詞

科学英語の特徴は3つのC、Clear(明瞭) Correct(正確) Concise(簡潔) で表せます。つまり同じ内容が伝わるなら、より少ない語数で表現する方が好ましいのです。そのための手段の1つが、名詞句と同じ内容をより簡潔に表現できる複合名詞です。

本文ではspaceに他の名詞をつなげた複合名詞が多数登場しています。

space travel 「宇宙旅行」　　　　　space mission 「宇宙探査ミッション」
space station 「宇宙ステーション」　　space anemia 「宇宙貧血」

また既存の複合名詞にさらに名詞を加えて、新しい複合名詞を作ることができます。
例えば、本文には以下のような例がありました。

blood cell 「血液細胞(血球)」　　　　　blood cell count 「血球数」

名詞句を作るときに悩まされる前置詞や冠詞が必要ない複合名詞は、英文を書くときに特に役立ちます。以下の例を見てみましょう。

宇宙飛行士のための規定食　diets for astronauts　→ astronaut diets
ミッションの目的　objectives of a mission　→ mission objectives

ここで1つ注意しなければならないことがあります。複合名詞では最後の名詞以外は、すべて単数形になるということ。最後の名詞以外の名詞が、形容詞としての役割をもつためです。上記の例で、名詞句では複数であるastronautsが複合名詞では単数のastronautになっているのはそのためです。

Exercise

次に示す名詞句から複合名詞を作りましょう。

例：an analysis carried out using X-ray → an X-ray analysis
1. a system for the purification of water　→ _____
2. a boat that is only used for pleasure　→ _____
3. a bottle used to contain perfume　→ _____

After You Read

A 会話を聞き、空所を埋めましょう。その後、会話をペアで練習しましょう。

Josh: Have you heard of space anemia?

Kate: What? I've never heard of it.

Josh: In space human bodies **¹**_____

_____ at higher rates than on Earth.

Kate: **²**_____?

Josh: They say it's due to fluid shifts **³**_____

_____ the weightless environment and back again. Having fewer red blood cells isn't a

problem when our body is weightless, **⁴**_____

_____, anemia becomes a serious problem.

Kate: I see. I hope they will find a way to treat it soon since **⁵**_____

_____ more popular.

B 以下の①と②の問題に答えましょう。

> 願望を表す **I hope** は実現してほしいと考えることを表す時に使います。**I wish**は実現不可能
> な願望を表します。このとき、現実とは反対の仮定、想像上の状況を述べるため、時制は一つ
> 後 (現在→過去、過去→過去完了) にずらします。

① 上記の説明と以下の例を参考にして、自分の言葉で文章の空所を埋めましょう。

　　ex) I hope they will find a way to treat it soon.「早くその治療法が見つかるといいなあ」

　　　　I wish I wasn't hospitalized.「入院してなかったらなあ」

　　I broke my leg in the accident.

　　⇒ I hope **¹**_____.

　　⇒ I wish **²**_____.

② I wishやI hopeを使いクラスメートとお互いの願望を語り合いましょう。

Behind the Scenes　　JAXAの解説による宇宙貧血

> 宇宙空間に滞在する宇宙飛行士の体内では体液シフトが起こり、上半身に体液が多く集ま
> ります。体液の量が多いと感知した体は、水分を腎臓から排出し、血液が一時的に濃縮状
> 態になります。血液が濃縮されると血栓などの危険性が高まるため、血液を薄めるために
> 赤血球の破壊が行われ、全体的な血液量が少なくなります。これが宇宙貧血と呼ばれる症
> 状で、無重力の環境に体が適応した結果とも言えるのです。(出典：JAXA 有人宇宙技術部
> 門ホームページ https://humans-in-space.jaxa.jp/faq/detail/000732.html)

12

１万年前に絶滅したマンモスを再び蘇らせようという計画がスタートしました。コロッサル（壮大な）と名付けられたこの計画が成功すれば、シベリアの風景が大きく変わるという期待がある一方、ジュラシックパークのようなこの計画には多くの倫理的ジレンマも存在し、そもそもこれを行うべきかについて科学者の間でも意見が分かれています。

" These Scientists Plan to Fully Resurrect a Woolly Mammoth within the Decade "

Before You Read

A 日本語の意味に合うように、空所に適切な語を語群から選んで書きましょう。語群には１つ余分なものがあります。

1. 科学者は長い間失われていたマンモスを復活させたいと望んでいる

scientists want to (   ) the long-lost woolly mammoths

2. これは、世界を大きく変えることになるだろう

it's going to (   ) all the difference in the world

3. 私たちのゴールは寒さに耐えるゾウを作ることだ

our goal is to make a cold-(   ) elephant

4. チームはマンモス様の特徴をもつ動物を作り出したいと望んでいる

the team hopes to create an animal with mammoth-(   ) characteristics

5. 彼らはマンモスの胎児を育てるための人工子宮の製造を計画している

they plan to (   ) an artificial uterus to grow the mammoth fetus

> like resurrect innovative resistant make create

B 下線部の英語の意味として適切な日本語を空所に書きましょう。

1. gene-editing technology   遺伝子編集（   ）

2. functionally equivalent to the mammoth   （   ）マンモスと同等な

3. long-extinct creatures   長い間絶滅していた（   ）

4. Jurassic-Park-style revival   ジュラシックパーク流の（   ）

5. still has major hurdles to overcome   まだ（   ）困難が待ち受けている

Reading

Notes

1 More than 10,000 years have passed since woolly mammoths roamed the planet, and a group of scientists wants to use gene editing technology to resurrect the long-lost creatures. A start-up named Colossal announced
5 yesterday that they have secured funding that could bring thousands of woolly mammoths back to Siberia.

roam 歩き回る

colossal 巨大な、壮大な

2 "This is a major milestone for us," says George Church, a geneticist at Harvard and the Massachusetts Institute of Technology (MIT), to Carl Zimmer for *The New York Times*.
10 "It's going to make all the difference in the world."

milestone 節目
geneticist 遺伝学者

3 Previous discussions on resurrecting long-extinct animals like the woolly mammoth have been largely theoretical, but Colossal has taken many of the first steps toward resurrecting the creature using a gene-editing
15 technology called CRISPR. Because woolly mammoths and Asian elephants shared a common ancestor some 6 million years ago, Church was optimistic that he could rewrite the elephants' DNA to produce something that looks and behaves like a mammoth using CRISPR, which acts as a copy-and-
20 paste tool for genetic code.

4 "Our goal is to make a cold-resistant elephant, but it is going to look and behave like a mammoth," Church says to *The Guardian*'s Ian Sample. "Not because we are trying to trick anybody, but because we want something that is
25 functionally equivalent to the mammoth, that will enjoy its time at -40 degrees Celsius."

trick たぶらかす

5 They compared genomes from surviving fragments of woolly mammoth DNA to those of modern elephants and pinpointed the biggest differences. By tweaking certain
30 genes to produce denser hair or a thicker layer of fat, the team hopes to create an animal with mammoth-like characteristics. Church and his colleagues plan to create an artificial mammoth uterus lined with stem-cell-derived tissue to grow the mammoth fetus. They are optimistic that

genome ゲノム、DNAのすべての遺伝情報

pinpoint
〜の位置を正確に示す
tweak p. 69 *l*. 48参照

stem-cell-derived
幹細胞由来の

74

they will produce an elephant-mammoth hybrid within the
next few years and hope to have a complete woolly mammoth
within the decade.

6 The team at Colossal says the project is about more than
a scientific stunt—the return of mammoths could benefit the
arctic landscape by reducing moss and increasing grassland,
according to *The New York Times*. Critics say there is little
evidence that mammoths would help, and instead
recommend more effective ways to restore the environment
than resurrecting long-extinct creatures.

7 "There's absolutely nothing that says that putting
mammoths out there will have any, any effect on climate
change whatsoever," says Love Dalén, a paleogeneticist at
the Centre for Paleogenetics in Stockholm, Sweden, to Katie
Hunt for *CNN*.

8 Even if Colossal can pull off the feat, the Jurassic-Park-
style revival has some scientists stopping to ask whether or
not they should do it at all. There are numerous ethical
quandaries around resurrecting extinct animals, especially
when scientists don't know very much about their biology and
behavior.

9 The team still has major hurdles to overcome before any
baby mammoths are running around the Siberian tundra,
including building an artificial uterus that can host a
200-pound fetus for its nearly two-year-long gestation period.

Notes	
hybrid	雑種
stunt	離れ技
paleogenetics	古遺伝学
pull off	成功させる
feat	p. 14 *l*. 15参照
ethical	道徳上の
quandary	困惑、当惑、板挟み
tundra	ツンドラ、凍土帯
gestation	妊娠（期間）

Extra Notes

l. 15 CRISPR：クリスパー（Clustered Regularly Interspaced Short Palindromic Repeatsの略）

Comprehension Questions

A 記事の内容に一致するものには T（True）、一致しないものには F（False）に丸をつけ、判断の基準になったパラグラフの番号を（ ）に書き込みましょう。ただし、基準とするパラグラフは複数ある場合もあります。

1. Every scientist desires the success of this Jurassic-Park-style revival of extinct animals.

T / F (　　　　)

2. Scientists will rewrite Asian elephants' DNA using CRISPR to produce something which looks like a mammoth.

T / F (　　　　)

3. A start-up named Colossal which aims to bring thousands of woolly mammoths back to Siberia has started funding, but nobody knows if they can collect enough money.

T / F (　　　　)

4. The goal of Colossal is to make a cold-resistant elephant that will help overcome the food crisis of Siberia.

T / F (　　　　)

5. Some people think that the return of mammoths will benefit the arctic landscape, but other people are critical of that idea.

T / F (　　　　)

B 以下は記事の要約です。適切な語を空所に書き入れ、音声を聞いて答えを確認しましょう。

DL 24　CD 2-40

　　　Woolly mammoths lived on this (**p**　　　　　　　¹) more than 10,000 years ago, but now scientists want to (**r**　　　　　　²) the extinct (**c**　　　　　　³). A start-up named Colossal has taken the first step toward the (**r**　　　　　⁴) of the animal using a (**g**　　　　　⁵)-editing technology called CRISPR. They rewrite the (**D**　　　　　⁶) of Asian elephants which shared a common (**a**　　　　　⁷) with woolly mammoths to produce something that looks and (**b**　　　　　⁸) like a mammoth. The mammoth fetus will be grown in an (**a**　　　　　⁹) mammoth uterus lined with stem-cell-derived (**t**　　　　　¹⁰). An elephant-mammoth (**h**　　　　　¹¹) could be produced within the next few years and a complete woolly mammoth within the decade.

Read Better, Understand More!

複合形容詞 1

2つ以上の名詞や形容詞をハイフンで結んで作った形容詞を複合形容詞と言います。

Clear（明瞭）Correct（正確）Concise（簡潔）が重要である科学英語では同じ内容を簡潔に伝えることのできる複合形容詞が大活躍します。

例えば本文では、形容詞の long（長い）に extinct、lost、two year が組み合わさってできた複合形容詞が使われていました。

long-lost 「長い間失われていた」　long-extinct 「長い間絶滅していた」
two-year-long 「2年間の」

その他本文に登場した複合形容詞には以下のものがあります。

cold-resistant 「寒さに耐性のある」　mammoth-like 「マンモス様の」
stem-cell-derived 「幹細胞から得られた」

「寒さに耐性のあるゾウ」を関係代名詞を使った名詞句で表現すると以下のようになります。

an elephant which is resistant to cold

これを複合形容詞を使って書くと、7語から3語に語数が減り、簡潔になります。

a cold-resistant elephant

また、通常語順が異なる英語と日本語が、複合形容詞では、語順が同じになるのです。つまり、ハイフンで結ばれた複合形容詞が登場したら、その順のまま日本語に直せばよいのです。

Exercise

複合形用詞を用いた下記の英文を日本語に直しましょう。

1. a silver-plated necklace _____
2. hydrogen-containing water _____
3. the best-selling book _____

After You Read

🅐 会話を聞き、空所を埋めましょう。その後、会話をペアで練習しましょう。

Sarah: Wow, Colossal has finally secured funding! ¹_____ how
　　　　it will turn out.

Daniel: What is Colossal?

Sarah: A start-up planning to ²_____
_____ to Siberia. They are going to rewrite Asian elephants' DNA using
　　　　genomes from surviving fragments of woolly mammoth DNA. The final goal ³_____
_____ mammoth-like elephant. Imagine baby
　　　　mammoths running around the Siberian tundra. How exciting!

Daniel: It sounds ⁴_____ Jurassic Park! I wonder if
　　　　they should do it.

Sarah: Well, the return of mammoths could benefit the arctic landscape. It will ⁵_____
_____.

Daniel: You are such an optimist!

🅑 以下の①と②の問題に答えましょう。

① 以下の例を見て、自分の言葉で文章の空所を埋めましょう。

　　　ex) Should they do it?「彼らはそれをするべきか」
　　　　　→ I wonder if they should do it.「彼らはそれをするべきかな」
　　　　　Who is the man?「あの男は誰だ」
　　　　　→ I wonder who the man is.「あの男は誰かな」

　　I got a present for you. I wonder ¹_____.
　　Eric is absent today. I wonder ²_____.

② ①で書いた内容を元にクラスメートと話し合いましょう。

Behind the Scenes　　CRISPR

CRISPRはClustered Regularly Interspaced Short Palindromic Repeatsの略で、細菌のDNAに
ある繰り返し配列のことです。1987年に九州大学の研究者らが発見しました。その後、米
仏の2人の女性科学者が、遺伝子の切断技術に応用したCRISPR-Cas9を開発し、2020年に
ノーベル化学賞を受賞しました。CRISPRは現在簡便で安価な遺伝子改変ツールとして、世
界中で利用されています。

UNIT 13

サシと呼ばれる霜降りの入った和牛肉はWagyuとして今世界中で人気です。大阪大学の研究者らは3Dプリンターを使い、和牛肉そっくりの培養肉の製造に成功しました。特定の品種の和牛の幹細胞から得られた生きた細胞を使い、筋繊維、脂肪、血管まで精密に再現されたこのお肉の味はまだ誰も試していませんが、将来温室ガスを減らす上で役立つことは間違いありません。

" Scientists Create First 3-D Printed Wagyu Beef "

▌ Before You Read

A 日本語の意味に合うように、空所に適切な語を語群から選んで書きましょう。語群には１つ余分なものがあります。

1. ３Dプリンターで作られた肉は、従来のやり方で育てられた牛肉の代替品になる
   3-D printed beef becomes an alternative to traditionally-(　　　　　　　　　　) beef

2. 和牛肉のあの美しいサシ、すなわち霜降り
   the beautiful sashi or (　　　　　　　　　　) of Wagyu beef

3. 和牛肉はその柔らかさと味のために珍重されてきた
   wagyu beef has been (　　　　　　　　　　) for its tenderness and flavor

4. 特定の和牛品種から得られた２種類の幹細胞
   two types of stem cells from specific (　　　　　　　　　　) of Wagyu cows

5. ３Dバイオプリンティングは生きた細胞を積み重ねて血管や筋肉組織を作りあげる
   3-D bioprinting (　　　　　　　　　　) living cells to build blood vessels and muscle tissue

> prized　raised　breeds　extract　stacks　marbling

B 下線部の英語の意味として適切な日本語を空所に書きましょう。

1. lab-grown meats　　　　　　　　　　(　　　　　　　　　　)肉
2. Wagyu's intramuscular fat content　　和牛肉の筋肉内脂肪(　　　　　　　　　　)
3. a perfect Wagyu cut was replicated　完璧な和牛肉の塊が(　　　　　　　　　　)された
4. tailor-made complex structures　　　(　　　　　　　　　　)複雑な構造
5. green-lighting eating the beef　　　　その牛肉を食べることを(　　　　　　　　　　)する

Reading

CD 2-42 ～ CD 2-49

Notes

1 Scientists in Japan successfully 3-D printed a cut of Wagyu beef that looks just like the real thing. The team at Osaka University in Japan used three dimensional bioprinting to replicate the cut's specific arrangement of
5 muscle, fat and blood vessels. They hope lab-grown meats could provide a more sustainable—and delicious—alternative to traditionally-raised beef.

bioprinting 生きた細胞や生体材料を用い、2D、3Dプリンターを使って、2次元・3次元の組織や臓器を製造するプロセス

2 "By improving this technology, it will be possible to not only reproduce complex meat structures, such as the
10 beautiful *sashi* [or marbling] of Wagyu beef, but to also make subtle adjustments to the fat and muscle components," study co-author Michiya Matsusaki said in a statement.

3 The study, published last month in *Nature Communications*, is the first to attempt bioprinting Wagyu
15 beef—an expensive cut prized for its tenderness, flavor and delicate fat marbling. Like traditional 3-D printing, bioprinting uses a computer-generated model that deposits layers of material to create a final three-dimensional object. But unlike standard methods which use materials like
20 plastic or metal, 3-D bioprinting stacks living cells to build complex structures like blood vessels and muscle tissue.

Nature Communications 生物学、物理学、化学、地球科学、健康科学等の分野の高品質な論文を出版するオープンアクセスジャーナル

4 This new beef isn't the first bioprinted cut of beef—an Israeli company unveiled their 3-D printed ribeye steak earlier this year—but Wagyu posed a specific challenge,
25 according to *Insider*'s Cheryl Teh. The team needed to recreate the Wagyu's signature intramuscular fat content, known more commonly as fat marbling or sashi.

Insider p. 45 *l*. 48参照

5 To create the manufactured meat, scientists used two types of stem cells from specific breeds of Wagyu cows,
30 reports Victor Tangermann for *Futurism*. By manipulating the stem cells, they could coax them into every type of cell needed to culture the meat. The individual fibers of muscle, fat and blood vessels were bio-printed in layers that replicated a perfect Wagyu cut.

manipulate 操作する、巧みに処理する
coax ~ into うまく（人）に～させる

35 **6** "Using the histological structure of Wagyu beef as a blueprint, we have developed a 3-D-printing method that can produce tailor-made complex structures, like muscle fibers, fat and blood vessels," study co-author Dong-Hee Kang said in a statement.

histological　組織学的
blueprint　設計図

40 **7** No one has tasted the beef, so the meat's flavor performance remains to be seen, reports Lauren Rouse for *Gizmodo Australia*. More studies are needed before anyone is green-lighting cooking or eating it. Because earlier experiments with cultured meats have grown largely

45 unstructured cuts, the team hopes this high-controlled printing method can improve lab-grown meat texture, too. Theoretically, a customizable meat printing method means scientists could create tastier, more tender cuts of beef than exist today.

Gizmodo Australia　ギズモード（最新テクノロジーやデジタル社会に関連するニュースを扱うテクノロジーメディアサイト）のオーストラリア版
high-controlled
高度にコントロールされた
customizable
カスタマイズ可能な

50 **8** The scientists hope their 3-D printed meat will be an appealing option for those looking to reduce their reliance on livestock, which currently accounts for around 15 percent of U.S. greenhouse gas emissions. Though lab-made Wagyu beef could be a more sustainable alternative to traditionally

55 raised meat, the high cost of production and limited regulatory oversight means it won't be available on supermarket shelves any time soon.

livestock　p. 39 *l*. 44参照

oversight　監督、管理

Extra Notes

l. 30 *Futurism*：ニューヨーク市を拠点とする、科学技術系のニュースやビデオを配信しているデジタルメディア企業

Comprehension Questions

A 記事の内容に一致するものには T（True）、一致しないものには F（False）に丸をつけ、判断の基準になったパラグラフの番号を（　）に書き込みましょう。ただし、基準とするパラグラフは複数ある場合もあります。

1. Scientists in Japan successfully 3-D printed a cut of Wagyu beef that tastes just like the real thing.　　　　　T / F （　　　）

2. Scientists could reproduce complex meat structures, such as sashi, but they have not yet made subtle adjustments to the fat and muscle components.　　　　　T / F （　　　）

3. Nobody has ever tried to bioprint a cut of beef before Japanese researchers at Osaka University.　　　　　T / F （　　　）

4. One of the merits of lab-made Wagyu beef is to reduce greenhouse gas emissions.　　　　　T / F （　　　）

5. According to Dong-Hee Kang, a 3-D-printing method can produce only simple structures.　　　　　T / F （　　　）

B 以下は記事の要約です。適切な語を空所に書き入れ、音声を聞いて答えを確認しましょう。

DL 26　CD 2-50

　　The first 3-D (**b**　　　　　　　¹) cut of Wagyu beef that looks just like the real thing was created. Researchers at Osaka University in Japan used 3-D bioprinting and (**s**　　　　　　²) living cells to successfully (**r**　　　　　　³) the cut's specific (**a**　　　　　　⁴) of muscle, fat and blood (**v**　　　　　⁵). Since (**l**　　　　　⁶) account for around 15 percent of U.S. greenhouse gas emissions, the (**l**　　　　　⁷) meats could provide a more (**s**　　　　　⁸) alternative to traditionally-(**r**　　　　　⁹) beef.

Read Better, Understand More!

複合形容詞 2

名詞句 meats which are grown in a laboratory は、複合形容詞を使うと本文3行目の表現 lab-grown meatsとなります。この例を参考に、複合形容詞の作り方を見ていきましょう。

手順1）名詞句先頭の名詞を後に移動する → which are grown in a laboratory meats

手順2）関係代名詞、Be動詞、前置詞、冠詞（句中にある場合）を削除する → grown laboratory meats

手順3）動詞の過去分詞形を名詞の直前に移動する → laboratory grown meats

手順4）複合形容詞をハイフンで結ぶ → laboratory-grown meats

次は、動詞の現在分詞の例 a plant which is producing oxygenを見てみましょう。

手順1）名詞句先頭の名詞を後ろに移動する → a which is producing oxygen plant

手順2）関係代名詞、Be動詞、前置詞、冠詞（句中にある場合）を削除する → a producing oxygen plant

手順3）動詞の現在分詞形を名詞の直前に移動する → a oxygen producing plant

手順4）複合形容詞をハイフンで結ぶ → an oxygen-producing plant

冠詞は名詞句のときの先頭の名詞の冠詞がそのまま残ります。ただし複合形容詞になると a → an などに変化することがあるので、要注意です。

もう一つ、形容詞を使った例 foods which are free from additives（添加物）をあげます。

手順1）名詞句先頭の名詞を後ろに移動する → which are free from additives foods

手順2）関係代名詞、Be動詞、前置詞、冠詞（句中にある場合）を削除する → free additives foods

手順3）形容詞を名詞の直前に移動する → additives free foods

手順4）複合形容詞をハイフンで結ぶ → additives-free foods

ちょっと待って！ここで一つ追加の説明があります。上のadditives（複数形）は単数形のadditiveに変える必要があります。その理由は、additivesは元の名詞句では名詞でしたが複合形容詞の中では形容詞となるためです。そこで、最終的には additive-free foodsとなるのです。

Exercise

次の名詞句を複合形容詞を使って書き換えましょう。

1. a suit made by a tailor　＿＿＿＿＿＿＿＿＿＿＿＿＿＿＿

2. a diode which is emitting light　＿＿＿＿＿＿＿＿＿＿＿＿＿＿＿

3. tissue which is derived from stem cells　＿＿＿＿＿＿＿＿＿＿＿＿＿＿＿

After You Read

A 会話を聞き、空所を埋めましょう。その後、会話をペアで練習しましょう。

Ann: Gee, **1**_____! According to

today's newspaper, this time they succeeded in bioprinting a cut of Wagyu beef.

Glenn: That's not new. I guess **2**_____

_____.

Ann: Oh, Wagyu beef is special. It has the beautiful sashi. In addition, they were able to

reproduce complex meat structures with **3**_____

_____ blood vessels.

Glenn: So, is it delicious?

Ann: No one has tasted the beef yet, but, theoretically, scientists can create tastier,

4_____.

Glenn: Hmm, **5**_____ a bite.

B 以下の①と②の問題に答えましょう。

① 以下の例を見て、自分の言葉で文章の空所を埋めましょう。

ex) They bioprinted a cut of Wagyu beef.「彼らは和牛肉の塊をバイオプリントした」

→ They succeeded in bioprinting a cut of Wagyu beef.「彼らは和牛肉の塊のバイオプリントに
成功した」

I succeeded in passing **1**_____. I can

2_____.

I succeeded in **3**_____ the job. I'm so glad

4_____.

I succeeded in **5**_____. I will

6_____.

② ①で書いた内容を元にクラスメートと話し合いましょう。

Behind the Scenes   3Dプリンターのいろいろ

レーザー光線をナイロンや金属粉末などに照射するSLS方式は、ジェットエンジン用部品
や医療用インプラントなどに、液体樹脂を紫外線で硬化させるSLA方式は、ハリウッド映
画の小道具製作などに使われています。またインクジェットプリンターのプリントヘッド
から紫外線硬化性の樹脂、着色剤、接着剤を吐出して、建築模型やフィギュア、医療の骨
モデルなどが製作されています。現在、消費者向けの3Dプリンターの主流となっている
のは、細いノズルの先端から溶解した樹脂を吐出し積層する、熱溶解積層方式です。

UNIT 14

スターウォーズの世界ではロボットは金属やセラミックでできていました。が、定義によれば、ロボットとは「人の代わりに何等かの作業を自律的に行う機械」のこと。昨年科学者はそれを生きた細胞で作り上げることに成功しました。さて、研究はさらに進み、今やこの生体ロボットは自らの子孫を生み出すようになったのです。

Scientists Unveiled the World's First Living Robots Last Year. Now, They Can Reproduce

Before You Read

A 日本語の意味に合うように、空所に適切な語を語群から選んで書きましょう。語群には 1 つ余分なものがあります。

1. 遺伝子改変されていないカエルの細胞から作られた生物
   an ( ) made from genetically unmodified frog cell

2. ツメガエルの属名のXenopusにちなみ「ゼノボット」と名付けられた
   named "xenobots" ( ) the clawed frogs' genus Xenopus

3. そもそもゼノボットを作り出すために、チームはスーパーコンピューターを用いた
   to create the xenobots in the first ( ), the team used a supercomputer

4. 培養した幹細胞を小さなピンセットと電極を用いて再構成した
   incubated stem cells were reconfigured using tiny ( ) and an electrode

5. このゼノボットは一定の条件でのみ生殖が可能であった
   the xenobots could only ( ) under specific conditions

> tweezers　reproduce　after　place　organism　pinchers

B 下線部の英語の意味として適切な日本語を空所に書きましょう。

1. <u>bundles</u> of stem cells　　　　幹細胞の（　　　　　　　　　）
2. the cells could even <u>self-heal</u>　これらの細胞は（　　　　　　　）すらできた
3. act on its own <u>on behalf of</u> people　人々（　　　　　　）自力で行動する
4. scooping up <u>free-floating</u> cells　（　　　　　　）細胞をすくい上げる
5. clean up environmental <u>contaminants</u>　環境（　　　　　　）を取り除く

Reading

	Notes

1 Early last year, a team of researchers announced the world's first living machines—bundles of stem cells from African clawed frogs (*Xenopus laevis*) that could be programmed to accomplish certain tasks. The sand grain–
5 sized cells could successfully move microscopic objects, whiz around Petri dishes and even self-heal, Katherine J. Wu reported for *Smithsonian* last year.

microscopic
微細な、極小の
whiz ビューっと走る

2 "Most people think of robots as made of metals and ceramics but it's not so much what a robot is made from but
10 what it does, which is act on its own on behalf of people," co-author Josh Bongard, a computer scientist at the University of Vermont, tells Katie Hunt for *CNN*. "In that way it's a robot, but it's also clearly an organism made from genetically unmodified frog cells."

on one's own
p. 14 *l*. 11参照

3 Since their original study, the team has been working to
15 harness the power of these tiny robots—named "xenobots" after the clawed frogs' genus *Xenopus*. In a new development, the team announced that xenobots can now reproduce in a way that is completely different from any plant or animal
20 known to science: by scooping up free-floating cells and assembling them into new clusters, Nicola Davis reports for *The Guardian*. The team published their findings this week in the journal *Proceedings of the National Academy of Sciences*.

harness 役立てる、利用する

Proceedings of the National Academy of Sciences
米科学アカデミー紀要

4 To create the xenobots in the first place, the team used a
25 supercomputer to create a blueprint for a new life form. With the design in hand, they collected stem cells from the frogs' embryos and incubated them before reconfiguring them Frankenstein-style using tiny tweezers and an electrode into
30 the shape designed by the supercomputer. The xenobots could then be programmed to complete certain tasks, and they've grown more complex since then, according to a press release.

blueprint p. 81 *l*. 36参照

embryo 胚

5 "One [xenobot] parent can begin a pile and then, by

chance, a second parent can push more cells into that pile,
and so on, generating the child," co-author Josh Bongard, an
expert in evolutionary robotics at the University of Vermont,
tells *New Scientist*.

[6] But the xenobots could only reproduce under specific
conditions. To make them more effective, the team used
artificial intelligence to test billions of different body shapes
and configurations on a supercomputer. Instead of a sphere,
it found that a Pac-Man-like, C-shaped bot was the best at
gathering individual stem cells in its mouth and bundling
them into new baby bots, *CNN* reports.

[7] Though this research is in its infant phases, the team
has high hopes for the xenobots. With further development,
they could be used in medicine—such as to help deliver
drugs within the body—or to clean up environmental
contaminants, *Smithsonian* reported last year.

[8] "There's all of this innate creativity in life," Bongard
says in the press release. "We want to understand that more
deeply—and how we can direct and push it toward new
forms."

Notes

evolutionary robotics
進化ロボット工学
New Scientist
p. 8 *l*. 13参照

configurations　構造

bot　ロボット

innate
本質的な、生まれながらの

Extra Notes

l. 3 African clawed frogs：アフリカツメガエル　卵が大きく手術が容易なので実験材料としてよく用いられる
l. 29 Frankenstein：英国人作家シェリーの小説に登場する人造人間。小説では触れられていないが、映画では死体を
切り取り、組み合わせ、電気を流して生命を与える描写がある。*l*. 43 Pac-Man：1980年にナムコがゲームセンター
用に開発した、迷路アクション型ビデオゲーム。丸いピザの一部が切り取られた形をしたパックマンが登場する。

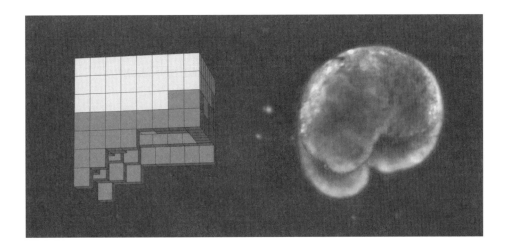

Comprehension Questions

A 記事の内容に一致するものには T（True）、一致しないものには F（False）に丸をつけ、判断の基準になったパラグラフの番号を（　）に書き込みましょう。ただし、基準とするパラグラフは複数ある場合もあります。

1. After having incubated stem cells from the frogs' embryos, the scientists reconfigured them Frankenstein-style into the shape designed by the supercomputer.

   T / F (　　　　)

2. The way xenobots reproduce is completely different from any plant or animal known to scientists. **T / F** (　　　　)

3. Xenobots are capable of moving independently and performing certain tasks for people, but they are not made of metals nor ceramics; therefore they are not robots.

   T / F (　　　　)

4. Last year, a group of researchers announced the world's first thinking machines that could accomplish certain tasks. **T / F** (　　　　)

5. This research being in its infant phases is not promising, since no one can think of its application. **T / F** (　　　　)

B 以下は記事の要約です。適切な語を空所に書き入れ、音声を聞いて答えを確認しましょう。

DL 28　　CD 2-60

Last year, researchers announced the world's first programmable living (**m**　　　　　　[1]). Xenobots, the (**b**　　　　　　[2]) of stem cells from African clawed frogs could (**s**　　　　　　[3]) move microscopic objects, whiz around and even (**s**　　　　　　[4]). It is an (**o**　　　　　　[5]) made from genetically (**u**　　　　　　[6]) frog cells, but it's a robot as it (**a**　　　　　　[7]) on its own on behalf of people.

The team (**c**　　　　　　[8]) stem cells from the frogs' embryos and incubated them before (**r**　　　　　　[9]) them using tweezers and an (**e**　　　　　　[10]) into the shape designed by the supercomputer. Xenobots can reproduce by (**s**　　　　　　[11]) up free-floating cells and (**a**　　　　　　[12]) them into new clusters.

Read Better, Understand More!

接頭辞・接尾辞 1

　一見知らない難しい単語に見えても、接頭辞や接尾辞を知っているとその単語の意味を推察することができます。接頭辞は語の前について新しい意味を加え、接尾辞は語の後につき品詞を変えます。

　本文に登場したmicroscopicを見てみましょう。

　これはmicroscope「顕微鏡」という名詞に、名詞を形容詞化する接尾辞-ic が加わってできた「微小の」という意味の形容詞です。このmicroscopicという形容詞にさらに接尾辞 -lyが加わると、microscopically「微視的に」という副詞ができあがります。-lyは形容詞を副詞に変える接尾辞です。

　さて、このmicroscopeという単語もよく見てみると、実は名詞のscope「見る器械」に micro(「微小の」という意味の接頭辞)が加わって作られているのです。接頭辞の例には、この他にも tele「遠い」、peri「周囲の」、oscillo「振動する」などがあり、それらがscopeに加わると、それぞれtelescope「望遠鏡」、periscope「潜望鏡」、oscilloscope「オシロスコープ」などの語ができあがります。

Exercise

次の単語に含まれている接頭辞や接尾辞を見つけ、それをヒントにその単語の意味を書きましょう。接頭辞や接尾辞は複数ある場合もあります。

1. scientific 　　　　接頭辞／接尾辞　(　　　　　　　　　　　)
　　　　　　　　　　　単語の意味は　　(　　　　　　　　　　　)

2. dramatically 　　　接頭辞／接尾辞　(　　　　　　　　　　　)
　　　　　　　　　　　単語の意味は　　(　　　　　　　　　　　)

3. unbelievable 　　　接頭辞／接尾辞　(　　　　　　　　　　　)
　　　　　　　　　　　単語の意味は　　(　　　　　　　　　　　)

After You Read

DL 29　　CD 2-61

A 会話を聞き、空所を埋めましょう。その後、会話をペアで練習しましょう。

Henry: Have you read the recent article ^{1} _____

_____ about the world's first living robots?

Emma: Living robots?

Henry: That's right. These tiny robots named "xenobots" are made of living cells. But they

^{2} _____ certain tasks on

behalf of people, just like ordinary ^{3} _____ .

Emma: You mean xenobots are man-made life?

Henry: Well, the article says the scientists reconfigured incubated stem cells Frankenstein-

style using ^{4} _____ .

Emma: For what purpose were they created in the first place?

Henry: Though they need further development, they could be used, for example, to clean up

microplastics in the sea, or for ^{5} _____

_____ .

B 以下の①と②の問題に答えましょう。

① 以下の例を見て、自分の言葉で文章の空所を埋めましょう。

ex) *Mother:* Do you have any plans for the evening? Karin is going to her friend's

birthday party tonight. But I must go to work from 4:00 p.m.

You: You mean I should drop and pick her up?

「つまり、私に彼女の送り迎えをしろってわけ」

Your friend: Do you like to ^{1} _____? I have two tickets for

a ^{2} _____ next Sunday. But, ^{3} _____ .

You: You mean ^{4} _____ ?

② ①で書いた内容を元にクラスメートと話し合いましょう。

Behind the Scenes　　ゼノボット

アフリカツメガエル（学名ゼノパス・ラエビス）の幹細胞から作られたのでゼノボットと名付けられたこの生体ロボットは、砂粒ほどの大きさですが、目標に向かって移動し、集団で作業をし、傷ついた箇所を自ら修復できるのです。バーモント大学の公式ニュースによれば、これはプログラム可能な生物で、将来は体内に薬物を送達するシステムである Drug Delivery System や、海洋のマイクロプラスチックの除去などへの応用も期待されるとのことです。

UNIT 15

その絵画の本当の作者は誰なのかを判定するのは鑑定士や美術史家の仕事ですが、近年、絵具の分析や、キャンバスへのX線照射などのテクノロジーがこの分野でも活躍しています。さて、今回登場するのは、極微細な領域のキャンバス表面の凹凸から、その絵を描いた画家を判別する新しいAIシステムです。

❱❱ New Tech Can Distinguish Brushwork of Different Artists

▌ Before You Read

Ⓐ 日本語の意味に合うように、空所に適切な語を語群から選んで書きましょう。語群には1つ余分なものがあります。

1. 特定の絵画の背後にいる本来の作者を美術史家が決定する助けになる
help art historians determine the (　　　　　　　　) creator behind particular paintings

2. このシステムは絵画の極小部分を分析し、筆遣いの違いを見つける
the system analyzes tiny sections of paintings for differences in (　　　　　　　　)

3. 一本の毛で塗られた絵の具がその芸術家の意図しないスタイルを示している
paint coming off a single (　　　　　　) is indicative of the artist's unintentional style

4. 物理学の学生と美術史家の間の共同研究の結果
a result of a (　　　　　　　　) between a physics student and an art historian

5. 学生は全く同じ絵筆、絵具、キャンバスを用いて黄色い花の絵を描いた
students painted yellow flowers using (　　　　　　　) brushes, paints and canvases

> collaboration　original　identical　brushwork　bristle　natural

Ⓑ 下線部の英語の意味として適切な日本語を空所に書きましょう。

1. <u>telltale</u> differences in brushwork　　　筆遣いの（　　　　　　　　）差

2. there is success in <u>sorting</u> the attribution　　　その帰属の（　　　　　　　　）に成功する

3. <u>break</u> the painting <u>down</u> into virtual patches　　　絵画を仮想の区画に（　　　　　　　　）

4. additional research not yet <u>published</u>　　　未（　　　　　　　　）のさらなる研究

5. a painting we have <u>an answer key</u> to　　　我々が（　　　　　　　　）を知っている絵画

Reading

1 A new artificial intelligence (AI) tool may be able to foil fraud and help art historians determine the original creator behind particular paintings. The system analyzes tiny sections of paintings, some as small as half a millimeter, for
5 telltale differences in brushwork, reports Benjamin Sutton for *The Art Newspaper.*

2 While previous projects used a form of machine learning to identify artists based on the analysis of high-resolution images of the paintings, the new system uses topographical
10 scans of the canvases.

3 "We found that even at the brush bristle level, there was a fair level of success in sorting the attribution," Kenneth Singer, a physicist at Case Western Reserve University, tells *The Art Newspaper.* "Frankly we don't really understand
15 that, it's kind of mind-boggling actually when you think about it, how the paint coming off a single bristle is indicative of what we're calling the artist's unintentional style."

4 The research is a result of a collaboration several years
20 ago between Michael McMaster, then a physics graduate student working with Singer, and Lauryn Smith, an art history scholar. With Singer and other colleagues, the pair published their findings last November in the journal *Heritage Science.*

25 **5** To test the AI system, four art students at the Cleveland Institute of Art each painted yellow flowers using identical brushes, paints and canvases, reports Steven Litt for *Cleveland.com.* The researchers scanned the surfaces of the paintings using a tool known as a chromatic confocal optical
30 profilometer, creating precise 3-D surface height data showing how the paint lay on the canvases, and digitally broke them into grids. The machine-learning system analyzed randomized samples and was able to sort them by the artist with a high level of accuracy.

Notes

foil 失敗させる
fraud ペテン、詐欺、不正

The Art Newspaper
アート・ニュースペーパー（イ
ギリスの美術月刊紙）

topographical
地形学的な、地理的な

physicist 物理学者
Case Western Reserve
University
ケース・ウェスタン・リザーブ
大学
mind-boggling
〈口語表現〉あぜんとさせる

Cleveland Institute of Art
クリーブランド芸術学院

Cleveland.com
オハイオ州のニュースを発信し
ているウェブサイト
chromatic confocal optical
profilometer 光を用いて表
面形状を測定する装置
surface height 表面高度
grid グリッド、位置を特定す
るために基準となる縦横の線
randomize ランダム化する

35 **6** "We broke the painting down into virtual patches ranging from one-half millimeter to a few centimeters square, so we no longer even have information about the subject matter," says Michael Hinczewski, another Case Western physicist and coauthor of the study, in a statement.

40 "But we can accurately predict who painted it from an individual patch. That's amazing."

7 In additional research not yet published, the team used the AI to try to distinguish original portions of the 17th-century painting *Portrait of Juan Pardo de Tavera* (1609) by

45 El Greco from sections that were damaged during the Spanish Civil War and restored later.

8 "This is a painting we have an answer key to, because we have photos of the destroyed painting and the current painting, so we're able to make a map of the areas that were

50 conserved, and [the AI] was able to identify those areas," Singer tells *The Art Newspaper*. "But there was another section of the painting that it identified as conserved that wasn't obvious, so we're going to have a painting conservator in Spain look at the painting to see what's going on."

conserve
保存する、保全する

conservator
保存管理 (修復) 者

Extra Notes

l. 24 *Heritage Science* : ヘリテージ・サイエンス誌。シュプリンガー社発行のオープンアクセスジャーナル

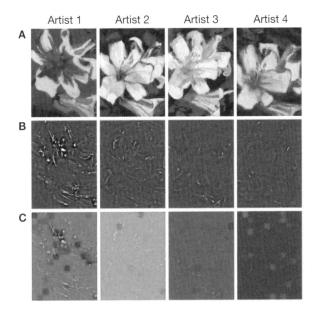

	Artist 1	Artist 2	Artist 3	Artist 4
A				
B				
C				

Comprehension Questions

A 記事の内容に一致するものには T(True)、一致しないものには F(False)に丸をつけ、判断の基準になったパラグラフの番号を（ ）に書き込みましょう。ただし、基準とするパラグラフは複数ある場合もあります。

1. Since there was an unexpected section of painting that AI identified as conserved, the researchers will ask a painting conservator in Spain to investigate that part of it.

   T / F ( )

2. The machine-learning system analyzed samples with 3-D surface height data and could determine very accurately which artist had painted the picture. **T / F** ( )

3. The new system uses a form of machine learning to identify artists based on the analysis of high-resolution images of the paintings. **T / F** ( )

4. The researchers fully understand how the paint coming off a single bristle is indicative of an artist's unintentional style. **T / F** ( )

5. The virtual patches obtained from the painting, ranging from one-half millimeter to a few centimeters square, lost information about the subject matter. **T / F** ( )

B 以下は記事の要約です。適切な語を空所に書き入れ、音声を聞いて答えを確認しましょう。

🎧 DL 30　⦿ CD 2-70

　　A new artificial intelligence system has been developed: it (**a**　　　　　¹) tiny sections of paintings, some as small as half a millimeter, for significant differences in (**b**　　　　　²) and determines the original creator behind (**p**　　　　　³) paintings. Different from conventional processes based on the analysis of high-resolution images of the paintings, the new system uses (**t**　　　　　⁴) scans of the canvases to (**i**　　　　　⁵) artists. An experiment where (**f**　　　　　⁶) art students painted yellow flowers using (**i**　　　　　⁷) brushes, paints and (**c**　　　　　⁸) showed that the system could sort them (**b**　　　　　⁹) the artist with a high level of (**a**　　　　　¹⁰).

Read Better, Understand More!

接頭辞・接尾辞 2

　本文に登場したindicativeは、動詞 indicate「示す」に動詞を形容詞化する接尾辞 -ative が加わってできた「示して」という意味の形容詞です。

次の動詞

inform 「情報を与える」	imagine 「想像する」	innovate 「革新する」

にそれぞれ-ativeが加わると、以下のように形容詞になります。

informative 「情報の」	imaginative 「想像の」	innovative 「革新的な」

また、動詞に -ativeが加わると、名詞化することもあります。

alternate 「交互に起こる」	preserve 「保存する」	add 「加える」

にそれぞれ-ativeが加わると、以下のように名詞になります。

alternative 「代替案」	preservative 「防腐剤」	additive 「添加物」

　他にも、本文にはunintentionalという単語が登場しました。意図という意味の名詞 intentionに否定の意味をもつ接頭辞のun-と、名詞を形容詞にする接尾辞の-alが加わったunintentional は「意図的でない」という意味の形容詞となります。

　このように接頭辞は単語の意味を変え、接尾辞は単語の品詞を変えるのです。

Exercise

次の単語には共通に含まれている接頭辞があります。それぞれの接頭辞はどのような意味をもとの単語に付け加えているのか考えましょう。

1. antiaging / antistatic / antiwarming　　接頭辞　　　(　　　　　　　　　　)
　　　　　　　　　　　　　　　　　　　　　　接頭辞の意味は (　　　　　　　　　)

2. discontinue / discharge / disappear　　接頭辞　　　(　　　　　　　　　　)
　　　　　　　　　　　　　　　　　　　　　接頭辞の意味は (　　　　　　　　　)

3. premature / precaution / prepaid　　　接頭辞　　　(　　　　　　　　　　)
　　　　　　　　　　　　　　　　　　　　　接頭辞の意味は (　　　　　　　　　)

After You Read

DL 31　　CD 2-71

A 会話を聞き、空所を埋めましょう。その後、会話をペアで練習しましょう。

David: What are you painting?

Liz: I am copying the Starry Night of Vincent van Gogh.

David: Amazing! **1**_____! You can sell
it as genuine to a small museum and make a fortune.

Liz: No way! There is an artificial intelligence tool to foil fraud, so **2**_____
_____. The paint coming off a single bristle will be
3_____. A
small patch of 1 millimeter square can accurately predict who painted it.

David: Speaking of artificial intelligence, **4**_____
_____ which can **5**_____. After
uploading your portrait photo, you can download your portrait painted by Van Gogh, for
example. It's so amusing.

B 以下の①と②の問題に答えましょう。

> Aの最後のDavidの発言にあるamusingは動詞 amuseの現在分詞。この他にもさまざまな動詞の現在分詞形が、喜怒哀楽を表現するのに使われます。

① 上記の説明と以下の例を参考にして、自分の言葉で文章の空所を埋めましょう。

ex) You can download your portrait painted by Van Gogh. It's so amusing.
　　「ゴッホが描いた自分の肖像画をダウンロードできるよ。とても面白いよ」
　　Elly says she can't visit me tomorrow because of the snow. It's disappointing.
　　「エリーが雪のため明日は来られないという。がっかりだ」

I went to **1**_____ for the first time in my life. It is one of
the largest **2**_____ in Japan. It was
3_____.

② ①で書いた内容を元にクラスメートと話し合いましょう。

Behind the Scenes　　　画家の意図しないスタイルを微小領域から見つけ出す

> ゴッホの作品に見られる独特のうねるような荒々しいタッチは、作家の意図を反映しています。一方で絵筆をキャンバスに置くときの角度や筆遣いは、無自覚に描かれた結果、残されたものです。それを分析するため、絵画の表面の盛り上がり（表面高度）を精密に調べ、細分化して解析を行いました。その結果特徴を見分けることが難しい極小領域（0.5mmとは絵筆の毛の直径に相当）からも、筆使いの違いが見つかり、作者が判定できたのです。

Acknowledgements

All the materials are reprinted by permission of the copyright holders.

Text Credits

Unit 1

Need a Creative Boost? Nap Like Thomas Edison and Salvador Dalí

https://www.smithsonianmag.com/smart-news/the-first-stage-of-sleep-is-a-creative-sweet-spot-180979211/

Unit 2

Curly the Curling Robot Can Beat the Pros at Their Own Game

https://www.smithsonianmag.com/smart-news/curly-curling-robot-can-beat-pros-their-own-game-180975951/

Unit 3

Italian Scientists Create Rising Pizza Dough Without Yeast

https://www.smithsonianmag.com/smart-news/italian-scientists-create-rising-pizza-dough-without-yeast-180979793/

Unit 4

Plastic Waste Can Be Transformed Into Vanilla Flavoring

https://www.smithsonianmag.com/smart-news/plastic-waste-can-be-transformed-vanilla-flavoring-study-shows-180978046/

Unit 5

Gas Stoves Are Worse for Climate and Health Than Previously Thought

https://www.smithsonianmag.com/smart-news/gas-stoves-are-worse-for-climate-and-health-than-previously-thought-180979494/

Unit 6

This Mushroom-Based Leather Could Be the Next Sustainable Fashion Material

https://www.smithsonianmag.com/smart-news/this-mushroom-based-leather-could-be-the-next-sustainable-fashion-material-180979170/

Unit 7

Scientists Build an Artificial Fish That Swims on Its Own Using Human Heart Cells

https://www.smithsonianmag.com/smart-news/scientists-build-an-artificial-fish-that-swims-on-its-own-using-human-heart-cells-180979570/

Unit 8

Research Shows Checking Your Phone Is Contagious Like Yawning

https://www.smithsonianmag.com/smart-news/research-shows-checking-your-phone-contagious-yawning-180977673/

Unit 9

To Save the Corpse Flower, Horticulturalists Are Playing the Role of Matchmakers

https://www.smithsonianmag.com/smart-news/can-horticulturalists-save-corpse-flower-180976816/

Unit 10

Robot Jumps a Record-Breaking 100 Feet in the Air

https://www.smithsonianmag.com/smart-news/robot-jumps-a-record-breaking-100-feet-in-the-air-180980006/

Unit 11

Space Is Destroying Astronauts' Red Blood Cells

https://www.smithsonianmag.com/smart-news/space-is-destroying-astronauts-blood-cells-180979418/

Unit 12

These Scientists Plan to Fully Resurrect a Woolly Mammoth Within the Decade

https://www.smithsonianmag.com/smart-news/these-scientists-plan-to-fully-resurrect-a-woolly-mammoth-within-the-decade-180978655/

Unit 13

Scientists Create First 3-D Printed Wagyu Beef

https://www.smithsonianmag.com/smart-news/scientists-create-first-3-d-printed-wagyu-beef-180978565/

Unit 14

Scientists Unveiled the World's First Living Robots Last Year. Now, They Can Reproduce

https://www.smithsonianmag.com/smart-news/scientists-unveiled-the-worlds-first-living-robots-last-year-now-they-can-now-reproduce-180979150/

Unit 15

New Tech Can Distinguish Brush Strokes of Different Artists

https://www.smithsonianmag.com/smart-news/new-tech-can-distinguish-brush-strokes-of-different-artists-180979332/

┌─────────────────────────────────────┐
│   本書にはCD（別売）があります   │
└─────────────────────────────────────┘

Science in Progress
More Articles from Smithsonian Magazine's Smart News
最新の科学をスミソニアンで読み解く

2023年 1 月20日　初版第 1 刷発行
2024年 2 月20日　初版第 3 刷発行

編著者　　　宮本　惠子

発行者　　　福岡　正人

発行所　　株式会社　金星堂

（〒101-0051）　東京都千代田区神田神保町 3-21
　　　　Tel.　（03）3263-3828（営業部）
　　　　　　　（03）3263-3997（編集部）
　　　　Fax　（03）3263-0716
　　　　https://www.kinsei-do.co.jp

編集担当　稲葉真美香　　　　　　　　　Printed in Japan
印刷所・製本所／倉敷印刷株式会社
本書の無断複製・複写は著作権法上での例外を除き禁じられています。本書を代
行業者等の第三者に依頼してスキャンやデジタル化することは、たとえ個人や家
庭内での利用であっても認められておりません。
落丁・乱丁本はお取り替えいたします。

ISBN978-4-7647-4185-0　C1082